HACKER REPUBLIC

DARK SIDE OF CYBERWORLD

FABIO GHIONI

Codice ISBN: 1-5207-3250-3
ISBN-13: 978-1-5207-3250-3

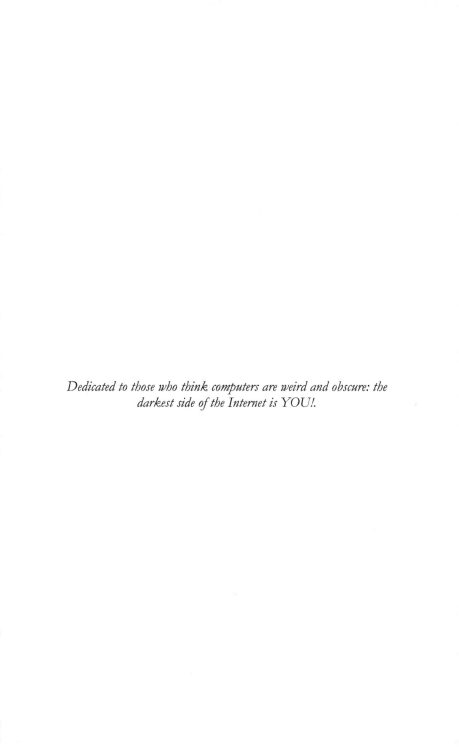

Dedicated to those who think computers are weird and obscure: the darkest side of the Internet is YOU!.

CONTENTS

To my best friends, partners and above and beyond....

PREFACE

HOW MANY people could have imagined that from cold and hardly populated Sweden could spawn a book that, while raising the curtain on the dark side of the local system, at the same time lifts another one that is much bigger, which includes all of human society? In his *Millennium* trilogy, Stieg Larsson actually achieved that and more, venturing a solution to all the evils that smacks of occult resistance, a partisan for some, subversive for others.

According to Larsson, the solution to the world's evils does not lie with the institutions, often corrupt and made of corruptible men, or with journalism, which is corruptible too and frequently factious, but with the initiative of a few individuals who break the rules, raising the level of the game to heights that many consider only science fiction.

Of course, institutions are also made of people who are very honest and dedicated to upholding the law, with a clear vision of what is good and what is not. However, there are few tools available to them and they are often made rigid by the same regulations that are supposed to act as guidelines. Likewise, there are also journalists dedicated to the truth without compromise, but civil servants and journalists are increasingly playing on a field where the enemy can be inside and outside, above and below them, with their realizing it before it is too late.

This is how the story of Millennium begins, with a man seeking the truth at all costs, a journalist who attempts to discover secrets, without the defenses that would allow him to come out of it unscathed. Policemen, secret service agents, top men in medicine, and judges play on a field where the enemy, like a virus, has replicated itself, eating the tissue of the system that they defend.

Then the warrior enters the stage, in this case a female warrior. From a certain point of view, Lisbeth is the symbol of all that they fight against but she is their only hope of reaching the truth and the solution to everything. She is a necessary and indispensable evil in times of war, and only through her action – whose only limit is her very personal code of honor – can evil be fought and defeated.

With Lisbeth, Stieg Larsson creates a very precise profile of the dark warrior who in this century must be the master of what is quickly conquering the world: technology.

Stieg Larsson passed away before he was able to narrate Lisbeth's future exploits, but he left many with the taste of what might have been and how many other evils Lisbeth Salander would have been able to unveil to the entire world, applying her very private law of retaliation: becoming the equivalent of a karmic agent for all those who ruin the world with greed and hate.

Organ traffic, white slavery and the trading of human beings, eugenics, experiments with drugs and psycho-pharmaceuticals are only some of the great evils that Lisbeth, through the Internet, would have been able to unveil.

Lisbeth's exploits already narrated by Larsson are only the stimulus for this book, providing the reader with a detailed explanation of how our heroine uses her skills and technology, aware that everyone of us, deep down, at least once in life, has wanted to be like her, or has wanted to destroy her.

Whoever of the two you may be, from whatever side of the fence you are on, there is one thing you need to know: there will always be a Lisbeth who in the solitude of her awareness, scorning all the risks, will fight our battles for us, even when we would like to burn her, and those like her, at the stake.

Finally, I must warn you about something. This is not a book on the *Millennium* trilogy nor a monograph on the character that has made it special, Lisbeth Salander. The ventures of whom by now has become the world's most famous hacker have been only a stimulus, an unexpected cue to introduce several truly important issues on the unknown world of underground hacking, and to what extent this can touch and influence the increasingly populous "Internet Nation" that we have christened as Cyberworld. The new inhabitants of this virtual dimension are for the most part happy navigators attracted by the promise of a rich land without borders, but completely ignorant of its dangers and without technical skills that allow them to read and completely understand the warning: "Mine field! Enter at your own risk."

The purpose of this book is to be a starting point for those who have already stepped foot in this world and for those who are feeling the inevitable attraction, not to fear it or reject it, but to raise their guard and focus their attention, and to pass on some defensive tricks, through an understanding of the general profile of a race of predators who move in the dark, of who they are, their motivations, the weapons available to them, and the main fundamentals of the rules of the game and the techniques used, based on one fundamental principle: know your enemy.

But those who instead feel the attraction of the "dark side", whose thirst for knowledge is instrumental to domination, to doing damage, to the greed for secrets and money, will probably be disappointed by both this book and by Lisbeth who, according to the rules of her world, in the end keeps the real secrets to herself.

GENESIS: LISBETH'S BREED

IT all begins as a voyage, an asymmetric voyage that is, with no regard for a timeline that Lisbeth is forced to impose on her life, or even for the law of cause and effect or the Vulcan logic handed down to us by too many episodes of *Star Trek*. Some ancient philosopher said that the voyage is the only thing that is really important and not the destination or the mission that our mind pretends to formulate as an excuse. Well, let's say that Lisbeth's story is one of a predestined woman who came into the world with extraordinary attributes and talents, but only potentially, in expectation that life would find a way to bring them to the surface and show them the light, opening the trapdoor that restrained them. But life or, if you prefer, destiny always finds a way to make everything more interesting and undetermined, and so – like the fiendish genie of the lamp gifts immortality inside a tomb or the infinite wealth in the icy Antarctic – Lisbeth receives her gift from pain, an inspirational pain that gives her the strength of a survivor and the form of a powerful and lone predator, but not one who feeds on meat, rather on secrets.

The pain activates everything, it does not matter if this also includes the vulnerabilities that have shaped those people who have truly meant something for the world and who, by some measure, have contributed to shaping its future, beating the collective resistance to change.

We should never doubt that every extraordinary attribute has its dark side or, perhaps better, that it comes with a very high price. And though this price should always be paid by those who have crossed paths with the one who has borne such a heavy burden, in the end it is always paid by the "predestined" one. And the required currency is the pain of living in a world that is not ready to accept a different energy and so it fights against it to isolate it and reduce it to impotence.

Lisbeth is the Hero, the hero who unfortunately only exists in comic strips and in the imagination of those who have one, the Hero who, in order to survive, must try to shut herself up in a container, that with difficulty manages to hold only that part which represents the public and social interface, with which she attempts to create a semblance of normality indispensable to survival in a community of other human beings.

But so what is visible to everyone is only a simulation, a mask put on intentionally, and only a few manage to see through what is hidden on the other side, i.e. what makes an average person truly extraordinary. And what we see is something strange, almost alien to human nature and certainly impossible to name with conventional names. And what human nature cannot understand and name is always frightening, so frightening, much more than the unknown evil.

That's how Lisbeth was born, with something extra, and one day this something is unchained by the energy of pain and on that day the Hero is born.

An intense, strange and at times disturbing look. Intelligence beyond measure. A behavioral pattern on the threshold of madness when viewed by those who comprise normality. An propulsive energy impossible to totally channel and that most of the time finds its outlet in excesses that intimidate. A dedication to adventures even at the risk of her own safety and life. A tendency too often cultivated to reject this world that could lead to brilliant autism, in the desire to abandon life or in the exercise of free will, taking the difference as a sign that the

world must be fought against and used for one's own purposes, even scoring a point for Satan the tempter.
This era, dominated by hypertechnology, which has become to all effects an experimental and imperfect extension of our human faculties, is producing in reaction a new species: what by now is known as hackers is an expression of it, though the commonly used definition has almost nothing to do with what is being unleashed in the real world.
This "new species" is like an anti-body, a collateral effect of our era or perhaps, for those who believe in an intelligent world, a reaction of nature to what man has wanted to unleash when a strategic decision has been taken to make humanity dependent on technology in daily life and in every aspect of life.
The members of the new species are born with the attributes that we have described and with an activation code that is almost always pain, especially the pain caused by the rejection inflicted on them by society. Hence each one of these extraordinary individuals develops a resistance to human relationships and goes to where they cannot be judged, i.e. to the world of machines and the global network.
There they can be anyone and invulnerable. And through their own intelligence they learn to enter behind the artificial mask of the Internet to the point of convincing themselves that they are a real and omnipotent creative force. And like for all true superheroes, hackers too take on a name that represents their new identity, an identity that makes them powerful against the world and, like always for the superheroes in the movies and comic strips, each of them has a skill that stands out above all the others and that forces them to help each other in the fight against a world - often to the point of subversion - that tries to isolate them and crush them, but that is powerless to fight them when they are a community.
Here, then, is where Lisbeth, who on the Internet goes by the name of Wasp, plays out not only her talents, but also those of the entire global community of those like her. A great big democracy without hierarchies or bosses, with its own rules

and that cannot be deleted no matter how many of its tentacles are cut off. Its members can be anywhere, in institutions or in multinational organizations, in the cold and anonymous rooms of a data processing center or in a secret terrorism base or a dark basement. And when they are on the Internet they become something bigger and definitely impossible to contain.
Each of them has made a decision at a certain point of the reawakening process into a new life on the Internet that has projected them into the world of the "guardians of justice", according to entirely personal ethical rules. Or they have become the classical "bad guys" who, aware of their abilities, have decide to exploit them for fame or money. Here is an interesting detail about the world of hackers: in need there is no judgment; in other words, a hacker can equally serve the light or the dark side of the force because the ends always justify the means. Legality and the clumsy attempt by institutions and countries to regulate a territory without borders have produced a thriving Internet security market that internationally generates hundreds of billions in revenue by exploiting fear of the unknown operating skills of this new class of superheroes, without however saying that nothing can really be done. And this is partially due to the fact that many of the system's vulnerabilities are intentional and many members of this new species are recruited into the ranks of governments and institutions, criminal and terrorist organizations, or self-proclaimed free champions of "justice" who denounce and expose the powers that be in the world. But, behind the superhero's mask, each one of them, when they are on the Internet, is part of a community of brotherhood of different people and they voluntarily follow its rules.
This is the world of Lisbeth Salander, 27 years old, five feet of grit and with the sex appeal of a dark fetish star, tattooed, intelligent, lone, with many secrets, and most of all with a lot of pain behind her. In "real" life, she is Wasp and she moves in Cyberspace with the speed and dexterity of a superhero who on the Internet acquires all the attributes of divinity, for better and for worse. She has realized her potential and is born again

on the Internet, and she uses her "powers" and those of others like her to do what she believes is "the right thing": robbing bank deposits, discovering unavowable secrets in peòple's lives, tapping into conversations, stealing identities and personal data, and then disappearing without leaving a trace.
Our rules are worth nothing: we are in her world.

HACKER REPUBLIC

A COUNTRY WITHOUT BORDERS

IMAGINE just another day: wake up, shower, breakfast, coffee, then the day begins and you distractedly log on to the Internet as usual. You navigate, chat, write something on Facebook, respond to emails, perhaps you download some MP3s or a pirated movie trailer put up on eMule (not exactly legal to tell the truth) or something like that, performing the daily rituals. Or you have a bit of fun, navigating on some porn site and you enjoy looking at pictures and videos of people practicing exotic forms of kamasutra. No need to feel too ashamed, you have lots of company: 90% of Internet traffic is pornography.

Everything seems normal, then, a day begun just like another other day.

But maybe that is not really the case. If you experience an uncomfortable feeling of doubt in your stomach, look at your past and ask yourself. Did you ever step on the toes of the wrong person? Perhaps you made fun of someone that seemed to be a nobody. Or you exaggerated in flattering a boss, snatching a promotion or raise from a deserving co-worker. Or you bothered somebody that seemed to deserve it, taking

liberty to do so with sadistic satisfaction at a time that seemed appropriate only to you.
Well, don't feel so relaxed because you may have done something, anything, perhaps unaware, to the wrong person: a hacker, for example. And now the time has come to pay the piper. But be careful, you could pay your entire life.
Especially if the hacker, who in the collective imagination is a nerd-style lone wolf, decides to work in a team. This is what Lisbeth does.
Let's take it from the beginning.
Lisbeth was the victim of a bullet in the head and premature burial, but she is saved at the last minute by her friend Mikael, and she wakes up in a hospital bed under arrest, charged with homicide.
When she gets hold of her faithful palmtop again, through a doctor who offers her protection, she contacts her fellow citizens of *Hacker Republic* to whom she tells her story. The idea of vendetta begins to snake around among her "invisible" co-workers, seeking to settle the score. Hackers think big, even in the case of vendetta or retaliation, so the most daring proposals light up on Lisbeth's palmtop: one of the targets is even the Swedish government, its establishment, and its infrastructure.
The ideas proposed are, in order, a nuclear attack on Stockholm (catastrophe!), a bomb explosion (massacre!), or causing a blackout in Stockholm (a big pain for the economy and those afraid of the dark!). Don't be too alarmed about a nuclear bomb: at times hackers like to hear the "sound" of their threats, though often they are too smart to try it in the real world. However, acting on the power grid or other critical systems is a task that, with a bit of committed teamwork, could go right and achieve the desired result.
Lisbeth knows that these are not just empty words from her peers.
Every hacker, even the most intelligent and talented, knows the enormous potential of teamwork, if the team is made up of the right people.

Hacker Republic was a very exclusive club that grouped the best of the best, an elite that any armed forces would have paid enormous sums to use for cyber-military purposes, provided that it was possible to induce citizens to display that kind of loyalty to a government. But that was highly unlikely.

>>> The girl who kicked the hornet's nest , p. 384

In fact, the more a country is industrialized, the more it is dependent on information systems.

To be sure, Italy is a bit behind some others, but only because Italians have always strongly resisted change, with a strong tendency, however, to imitate US/UK models with a ten-year lag. Nonetheless, Italy too is adapting to the system, and very soon almost anything will able to get done through the Internet or a special information system. The new industrialization is already like that in the US, in most British Commonwealth countries, in Japan, and in almost all east Asian countries.
A lot of "sensitive" data on identity, assets, health, legal cases, and the like, is already in databanks, though often paid for. In some countries, like Brazil and Estonia, even the electoral system is completely electronic. And remember that, any time you execute transactions on the Internet or through an electronic system (for example, when you use a supermarket membership card to pile up points or a public transportation ID card), a databank records your transaction and this will never be deleted, and it will be on a computer linked to the Internet or available to someone who sooner or later will want to find it.
But that's not all. All the vital sectors for the functioning of a country and its economy are entirely managed on information systems, aptly called "critical infrastructure", whose food chain begins with electricity, without which nothing would work and we would return to the Middle Ages. This is true for

telecommunications, without which the economy's speed of interaction and progress would slow drastically. In the same way, this is also true for other sectors, like transport, defense, water resources, food, banks, and so on.
Let's take electricity for example: generation, purchase, storage, and distribution are regulated and planned by computers which are increasingly connected, directly or indirectly, to the Internet. Well, all the world's web computers have a similar configuration, exactly like it is for people: though everyone is different, the structure of their bodies is identical. The same is true for the peripheral equipment that allows these systems to communicate. First we have hardware, which is made up of five fundamental components: (i) equipment that processes and interprets information, (ii) that stores the information (e.g. hard disks), (iii) that manages person-to-machine interface, (iv) that powers the system, and (v) that manages outside interface, allowing the machine to communicate with other machines and links it with machine networks.
Then there is software, mainly stored on the hard disk. There are three main types of software: (i) operating systems, which allow the machine to start up, function, and interact with people or with other machines, (ii) applications, which allow people to process information in many different ways and to use the computer to communicate with other people, and finally (iii) data, i.e. all the information that before computers was written on paper and printed on film or recorded on tape.
So software governs everything, and it also manages communications and interaction with the human world. All software systems, and I mean all, have one or more vulnerabilities and it is exactly these vulnerabilities that hackers exploit.
It is useful to explain one of the reasons for these defects: to sustain constant earnings growth, companies continue to produce new technologies or upgraded versions of the same technology. However, they think that they do not have time to test them well, so consumers are the ones who do the testing for them and then, little by little, as the bugs and defects come

out, the software companies release so-called patches that here and there fix some of the problems detected after the product is first released. But be careful: often the patches are symptomatic, like pain-killers, i.e. they act on the symptoms and not on the cause, and often, just like drugs, they have side-effects. Finally, before they get around to making a stable version of a system, they come out with another one, and the cycle continues.

It is still not clear whether this imperfect-systems policy is intentional, but the fact is that numerous software defects are one of the two factors that allow hackers to dominate the Internet. The second system weakness that information system pirates exploit is the human factor. And Lisbeth knows something about it.

It is precisely our fragile and manipulatable psychology that has given rise to disciplines like social engineering or, the very latest, psychotronics, which exploits human weaknesses in relation to the new world created by the Internet, and the affirmed neurolinguistics programming (NLP) which teaches how to manipulate the brain's response to certain stimuli. NLP is heavily used in sales training programs. If we really want to be precise, perhaps the first type of hacker is the one that began to exploit human weakness. One of the greatest examples, as well as pioneer of the modern era, is a figure no less than Lavrentij Berija, founder of the KGB and of "psycho-politics", the basis of training for Soviet agents groomed to infiltrate NATO countries and manipulate and control key people to get them to reveal secrets or involuntarily commit homicide.

However, the fundamental human weakness is stupidity, which is an observable feature in people of all ages, races, and genders. In the majority of cases it is stupidity in good faith. In the second volume of the trilogy, Lisbeth exploits, so to speak, the unconscious diligence of the district attorney Elkström who brings his work home, breaking office rules and thus compromising all of the system's defensive procedures.

The author's conclusion is absolutely the right one:

Once again this proved the thesis that no security system is better than the most stupid of its operators.

>>> The girl who played with fire, p. 492

So the systems that manage a country's electricity can be attacked without great difficulty. And do not think that a hacker's only purpose is to cause damage. A hacker's real objective is to "own" a system and leave a sleeping Trojan Horse in it, recallable on command in case of need. The biggest problem is not staying in the dark. One of the most vulnerable objects is the meter, that nice little device that electric companies can now read remotely. One day you may be in the position of having to apply for a mortgage to pay the electric bill: are you sure that you can prove that you are not the person who consumed all that electricity?
Islamic terrorists and militant groups in persistently unstable countries organize hacker divisions, in part because it is too easy to attack Western-block countries through the Internet. Do you remember that in 2003 the United States and Europe were hit by a series of black-outs? That year Italy too was hit by one, but the cause was attributed to a tree that fell on a pylon. Do you think that if it had been the work of a team of hackers the news would have been reported?
So, when Lisbeth's friend propose shutting down the Swedish government, they know that they have a chance of actually doing it.
Those who read the novels know that the girl will not fall into temptation, but it hardly matters. My point is to emphasize that the more an institution is dependent on technology, the more its vulnerability increases. In other words, it is more difficult to infiltrate paper archives, stored in an office basement, than a digital databank. Strange type of progress.

If fifty of the world's best hackers were to decide to launch a joint attack against a government, the

government would probably survive, but not without damage. The cost would be calculated in billions if Lisbeth had given thumbs down. She thought about this for a little while.

>>> The girl who kicked the hornet's nest, p. 385

HOW TO RUIN THE LIVES OF THOSE WHO DESERVE IT

While she was reading the *Hacker Republic citizens'* proposals on encrypted chat to retaliate against Sweden, Lisbeth remembered a similar episode in defense of a fellow citizen.

A few years before a Hacker Republic citizen, who in civilian clothes was a California programmer, was robbed of a patent by a rampant dot.com company which even had the balls to sue him for it to boot. As a result, all Hacker Republic citizens focused extraordinary energy on abusively entering into every computer owned by the company with the mission of destroying it. All business secrets, every e-mail - together with several faked documents that proved that the company's chief executive was involved in tax fraud - were put on the Internet together with information on the chief executive's secret lover and pictures from a Hollywood party in which he was sniffing cocaine. The company went bankrupt in a few months and years later some members of the Hacker Republic National Guard were still busy tormenting the former CEO.

>>> The girl who kicked the hornet's nest,, p. 385

Justice is done: revenge was taken for the good guy and the badguy paid a very high price for his wrongdoing, losing everything he had, including his reputation.
What do you say?
With their complex way of conceiving of "justice", the hackers decided to react in a coordinated fashion to restore balance, despite their individualistic nature. Though gathering in virtual communities, they develop a tendency towards extreme individualism and, fed by the power that they objectively wield over Cyberworld, outsized egocentrism that leads them to attack their own kind, but only if one dare think of himself as better than the rest.
So how complicated is it for Lisbeth and her friends to infiltrate the systems of a dot.com company? As we have seen, if it is online and does not use "alien technology", it is a rather simple undertaking.
All these systems and their vulnerabilities are published in accessible bulletins: just look up the system's name and "vulnerability" as key words on a search engine and a good hacker can do it. There are dozens, even hundreds, of mailing lists and technical discussion forums that focus solely on finding faults and making them known, with the aim of forcing software companies to come out with their famous patches. At times some of these sites even make available software that directly exploits the weaknesses found.
Lisbeth is lucky because she can count on the help of a lot of hacker friends located throughout the world. The Internet is to all effects a parallel world, but with a significant difference: no borders, and so no jurisdiction. Lisbeth and her fellow "citizens" know well that, for as "right" as it may be, any action they take is considered criminal by law in almost every country in the world.
Since one of the fundamental rules, then, is not to act in one's own jurisdiction, outside help is essential. While it is true that

there are Internet infiltration systems that allow a hacker access to a computer by making it believe that the activity originates in some far and exotic country, in fact he is close to home. Nonetheless, the better the hacker, the more he is a true professional, and the more paranoid he is, the more he knows that there is always a possibility, however remote, that someone just as motivated and as good as he is could get to him.

You will ask whether this kind of thing actually happens in real life.

Well, it does happen. To tell the truth, however, it is hard to be lucky like the citizens of Hacker Republic, but what can happen in the real world at times goes beyond your worst nightmares.

Here are a few examples.

Infiltrating a company's network is not only doable, it is rather easy even for people who are not highly skilled; however, it is almost impossible to find a company that has information pertaining to illegal activities on its computer. You might discover operating documents, perhaps strategic or sensitive business content, but no one would be so stupid as to keep information about fraud or tax evasion or accounting tricks on his computer or on company computers accessible to all employees. Recalling Lisbeth's philosophy, every individual, no matter how honest he seems, has at least one unavowable secret, all you have to do is find it. In this story, hackers merely restore natural equilibrium, exposing the bad, revealing their infamous secrets, and publishing them on the Internet.

Perhaps in the victim's email there are references to an affair. It is rather common for naive people to manage their extramarital relations via email, using company PCs. Following different leads, but inspired by the same philosophy, it is easy to uncover the illicit vice of sniffing cocaine. In this case the proof must naturally be in the form of pictures. There are two ways: either you follow the cocaine sniffer and take a picture while he's doing it, or you get proof through a professional on the scene. In this case the pictures were obtained via access to an exclusive Hollywood party. You may recall that hackers do not act only on the Internet, on the contrary. A good half of what they do is in the realm of social engineering. In this case, the hacker treats a person exactly as he would treat a computer that he wants to infiltrate. Imagine being his target: first he will look for you on the Internet, on open sources, everything that is published about you, in an effort to deduce your psychological profile and all your weaknesses, digging into what you have written in various forums and mailing lists. He will explore and analyze your profile on social networks like Facebook, MySpace, Naymz, Twitter, Linkedin, etc., perhaps seeking a direct link with you through a false identity to become more intimate with you.

When he knows your tastes, your dreams, your fantasies, disappointments and hopes, i.e. what makes you tick, perhaps he may already know enough to send you an initial torpedo. If that is not the case, then he will try in public databanks, and rest assured that within a few years almost everything that there is to know about a person will be accessible on the Internet. This is already the case in the United States where there are even companies whose primary business is to gather information on citizens, from all the public databanks, and make it available, for pay naturally, to whoever is interested in it. And I am not talking about basic information like, first name, last name, date of birth, but your education, work, tax and criminal records, etc. Perhaps you have a supermarket loyalty card which – and they already do – records even the purchases you make, or one from your favorite bookstore. To be sure, a hacker will always first try to obtain such information on his own, but if he does not succeed, be sure that he will be willing to pay to get the information that he needs. If he is very meticulous and he really wants to ruin you, he will reach the point of following you, of going through your garbage, of buying your telephone print-outs from some friend or hacker that has access to your telephone company's system and anything else that is indispensable and humanly and technically feasible.

When the hacker manages to uncover your contact information, for example your email address and the IP address from which you access the Internet, he will use one of any number of infiltration techniques to access your computer and install a Trojan Horse. One of them is called Asphyxia, the software that Lisbeth and Hacker Republic use to control other computers through the Internet and suck from them all the information contained on the hard disk: an apparently simple tool, but incredibly powerful, it is the real trick up Ms. Salander's sleeve, who makes unrestrained use of it as the story unfolds. Using this program, Lisbeth first earns a living browsing through other people's computers on behalf of the investigator Armanskij. Then she gets rich at the expense of the mafioso businessman Wennerstörm, she finds a bothersome stalker in the first stages of his development, she monitors the life of the attorney Bjurman to prevent him from ruining the lives of other women like her, she takes control of the computer of the attorney general who is investigating her, and of the entire Swedish police, etc.
But that's not all. If the hacker knows your physical address, he or one of his contacts will certainly make a trip to your house to check whether you have a Wi-Fi access point and, if you have and the security on it is the standard one, be sure that he will "own" you very shortly.
This tool that Lisbeth and the citizens of Hacker Republic use in information system terms is called Trojan Horse. In short, it is a virus whose only mission is to make your computer totally available to the hacker: once infected, he can take total control over it, making it act at his command, perhaps even against other PCs on the internet, infecting them in turn. Computers whose operating system is a version of Windows are the most vulnerable because, since they are so widespread, they are hackers' preferred targets. In 2000, a group similar to Hacker Republic, named Cult of the Death Cow (CdC), packaged one of the very first and most famous Trojan Horse, naming it Back Orifice instead of Asphyxia. After having exploited it to the max, they made a spectacular demonstration of it during

one of the most famous hackers' conferences, held in Las Vegas in 2000. Perhaps Lisbeth was there.
Since then, every hacker organization has built its own weapons. And remember, by the time any of those tools become public, they are already useless to them.
However, Liz and her partners have developed a real weapon capable of infecting any type of system out there. Let's not delude ourselves that an antivirus or local firewall can be of any use. At best, these protection systems could bother a hacker a little bit, but that's it. Normally antivirus programs are designed against weapons that are already known and regularly used by wannabe hackers, i.e. those that have neither the guts nor the talent to be real hackers, but indulge themselves by downloading tools from the internet and trying to make a name for themselves as hackers. A true hacker knows his mission well and does not use standard tools.
If the hacker's mission is to find specific information on your computer, the best way to do it is to instruct the Trojan Horse to download the entire hard disk on the Internet, normally on a server and at an address in some exotic country, exactly like Plague did on Lisbeth's behalf.

Mikael deactivated ICQ and entered into The Riders. Everything he found was a link from Plague to an anonymous address that consisted only of numbers. He copied the address on Explorer, hit enter, and immediately entered a homepage somewhere on the Internet containing the 16 gigabyte comprising the hard disk of attorney general Richard Ekström. Evidently, Plague made life easy by copying Ekström's entire hard disk. Mikael took an hour to go through its content. He deleted system files, programs, and an endless quantity of preliminary investigations that seemed to go on for years back in time. In the end he downloaded four folders. He named three of them IndPrel/Salander, Salander/Waste, and IndPrel/Nieiermann. The fourth folder was a copy of attorney general Ekström's email up to two o'clock the

day before. Thanks Plague.

>>> The girl who kicked the hornet's nest, p. 457

It takes some time to download an entire hard disk, but you can instruct the Trojan Horse to do it only when the victim is not using the PC so as not to raise suspicion. Afterwards, the Trojan Horse is normally instructed to check once a day if there are any changes to files, in which case it sends only added or modified files to an address set by the hacker. The hard disk also contains all the passwords saved by the system, as well as fundamental information for sites where you input credentials, such as Facebook, your remote email, your online bank account, your remote company connection, etc. At his convenience, the hacker can later search for the information that he needs, while in the case of passwords, he can comfortably crack the cryptography that hides them by starting a program that tries thousands of passwords per second and letting it run until it finds yours.

But not too many people know that one of the best ways of installing a Trojan Horse is to have the PC physically in your hands. It doesn't matter if it's turned on or off, or if it is protected by a password.
In the second volume of the trilogy, Stieg Larsson talks in sufficient detail about the operations that Lisbeth executed to access the hard disk of her former employer Armanskij. In this case, Lisbeth accesses the computer and instructs it to start up directly from the CD that, among other things, contains a basic operating system (Windows XP, Linux, Ubuntu, etc.) and she uses it only to install the Trojan Horse – the notorious Asphyxia – or to position it so that the user himself installs it the next time he starts up the system. Today the same operation can be executed by using a USB pen drive with a large capacity, while for desktop PCs some really special cables are sold for keyboards: short extensions that are applied when you are not there and removed a day later.

They contain a small memory unit that records everything that you type on your keyboard, including passwords. The hacker can then download the data and have what he needs to access not only your computer, but also everything that you have access to, comfortably from his own home. So be careful about leaving your PC exposed in your office or hotel room.
Finally, be careful about anyone who asks you: "Can I use your PC for a minute? I only have to check my email", because that's how he can take control of it. It will only take him an instant to download the virus directly from his pen drive or from a web address that he has set up for the victims that let him get his hand on their computer.
You've already let it happen, right?

When she finished, she took out the CD and restarted the computer with the new version of Internet Explorer. The program appeared and behaved exactly like the original version, but it was a bit bigger and it was a microsecond slower. The rest was identical to the original, including the installation date. There was no trace of the original file.

>>> The girl who played with fire, p. 132

To tell the truth, it will be very difficult for a hacker to install a Trojan Horse that replaces Internet Explorer because it is almost certain that one of Windows' functions that controls the integrity and authenticity of the Microsoft software product would become aware of it and restore the original. The most effective Trojan Horses are the simplest ones. If a hacker wants, he could program one of them that allows him to do things remotely, like open and close the CD reader's window or other irksome things like that. But for what purpose? A Trojan Horse is more powerful the more invisible it is and the less it disturbs the host system. There are cases where Trojan Horses allow access to an embedded videocamera or microphone, but these are very special situations where it is it

important to monitor the environment surrounding the computer rather than have access to data.
But that is why you should always deactivate the microphone when you are not using it, and once in a while look at the light signaling that the videocamera is activated, you never know…
As you can see, even the installation date (or file creation date on a PC) can be manipulated. On this subject, see the section "Your worst nightmare", but in the meantime imagine what could be copied from your PC without your knowing about it and in such a way that it seems you were the one doing it. Do you feel the chills?
Back on topic, once the Trojan Horse is installed, a professional hacker, who well knows that his PC must stay clean, will certainly not copy the hard disk there.

She input the ftp address of a server in the Netherlands and a command window opened. She clicked copy, wrote Armanskij/MiltSec, and clicked ok. The computer immediately began to copy Dragan Armanskij's hard disk onto the Netherlands server. A clocked told her that the procedure would take thirty-five minutes.

>>> The girl who played with fire, p. 132

Okay, here too we have to specify something important. For as liberal as the Netherlands is, it is still a European Union country and it is not exactly a brilliant idea to store stolen material, like a hacker does, on a server in an EU country. In the end, even if the hacker's underlying intentions are good, he is still committing an illicit act that, in the United States for example, is a very serious federal crime.
A professional hacker that needs space to store stolen data will source at least three servers in three different countries in jurisdictions that are far away from the EU or the United States, for example in Asia or the Middle East where the linguistic barrier acts as another filter.
If he is truly an expert, he will never succumb to the delirium

of omnipotence, but will always bear in mind that one day he could be in trouble and then he will not want all that he has gathered up to that time to fall into the hands of an investigation team. For this very reason, server space will also be treated with cryptography and, as Lisbeth arranged, the data will be recognizable and accessible only through a customized program like Asphyxia 1.3.

To be thorough, we have to say that hackers do not work only Windows systems. It is obvious that Windows software is the most common target of those seeking vulnerabilities, but in part because it is much more widely used than all the others. Normally, when dealing with systems other than Windows, the hacker prepares, or has someone prepare, a specific weapon for the mission that he must accomplish.

So it is true, then, that if you use a less widespread system, the chances that it can be attacked by a run-of-the-mill hacker surfing the Internet are very low, but this does not mean that you are safe from the hacker who is looking specifically for you.

Lisbeth, who is intelligent and very foresighted, had an Asphyxia developed also for Linux and MacOS systems, enabling her to infect also the computer of Mikael Blomkvist.

She ran a few errands in the afternoon and returned home around seven, she turned on her PowerBook and started up Asphyxia 1.3. The MikBlom/laptap icon was already on the server in the Netherlands. She double-clicked and opened the copy of Mikael Blomkvist's hard disk. It was the first time that she accessed his computer since she had left Sweden more than a year ago. She noted with satisfaction that he had not yet switched to the latest MacOs, which would have caused Asphyxia to be deleted, thus interrupting the bugging. But she thought that she would have to modify the program so that it would not be disturbed by any upgrading.

>>> The girl who played with fire, p. 207

What does Lisbeth do when she needs to penetrate a system, but it is physically impossible for her to do it herself?
She contacts a trusted person who is part of her network and, in this specific case, who is also a citizen of Hacker Republic, just like her. But it's not a question of a simple favor.

Attorney General Richard Ekström, who is responsible for preliminary investigations, lives in Täby. He's married, has two children, and he has a broadband connection at his house. I would need access to his laptop or else his home computer. I need to be able to read it in real time. Hostile takeover. She knew that Plague rarely left his apartment in Sundbyberg, but she hoped that he had trained some pimply teenager to do the work in the field. She did not sign the message, it would have been superfluous. She received the reply when she went back into ICQ fifteen minutes later.
What do you pay?
10,000 in your account + expenses and 5,000 for your helper.
I'll let you know.

>>> The girl who played with fire, p. 491

A hacker is able to communicate the most information in the fewest number of words, and this is an example of it. Let's put aside the small detail that here Lisbeth is ordering a hostile takeover of the computer of the attorney general that is investigating her and let's see what she is really asking Plague to do.
First of all, she told him that the house has a broadband connection, which means that his internet connection is certainly fast, allowing for the download of a large quantity of data in short time. Then there is the significant detail that there, besides him, there are at least three other people in the house who are his family members. This means that there is

presumably a Wi-Fi access point for the entire house and the entire family. To be sure, broadband providers almost always offer Wi-Fi access in houses, providing them with one access point. However, if this is not the case, the presence of three other potential users increases the chances of wireless access from outside and quadruples the probability of finding vulnerabilities to exploit.

The pimply teenager that Lisbeth refers to may compared to the pupil of a martial arts teacher. Some hackers "bring up" a young person to teach their skills to, like Plague had done with Lisbeth. This is not a rule, however, on the contrary, most professional hackers jealously safeguard their knowledge and do not have the slightest intention of passing it on.

With a Wi-Fi access point with a range of at least 90 feet, the pimply teenager and Plague himself would have easily been able to penetrate their victims' in-house network without being seen or traced. Today there is no impenetrable security for Wi-Fi networks, not even the latest generation WPA protocol.

Going back to our story, the attorney general regularly brought his work home and his household network had no protection. This is an easy game for the hacker, while the Justice Department has probably thrown a lot of money at security technology without thinking of prohibiting government attorneys from taking work home. This situation is too common.

Finally, the expression "hostile takeover" is quite useless in the context of requests among hackers: there are no known cases of information system piracy where the hacker asks the victims, "Excuse me, can I take control of your computer, install a Trojan Horse and read everything that you do, plus copy it in a secure place on the Internet?" Any takeover of a computer is a hostile takeover because it is done against the victim's will and consent, so for this very reason it can be defined as such.

HOW TO COMMUNICATE WITH A HACKER

If you know a professional hacker, you can be sure that he has your computer under control or, if for some reason he has not managed to access it, at least your email. Naturally if he is an employee of your company or a co-worker, he will certainly also monitor most other co-workers and he will certainly have obtained privileged access to the company's systems from outside. First, he will sniff out all possible credentials (usernames and passwords) of most of his co-workers, and then use them in later operations to consolidate his monitoring of the new territory.

Do not be alarmed, he does not do it with bad intentions. A hacker simply wants to keep the situation under control, just like Lisbeth did with Milton Security (her employer) and with Mikael Blomkvist (her friend and fellow adventurer). In short, to a hacker, control of territory means possessing the computers of the people that he deals with.

If by chance you have become aware of the presence of a hacker among your personal or work acquaintances, and you want to communicate with him only, you have a fast-track way of doing it: your computer.

Just leave a message on your PC's desktop and rest assured that, sooner or later, he will read it.

Dear Lisbeth,
I write you this letter leaving it on my hard disk, certain that sooner or later you will wind up reading it. I remember well what you did with Wennerström's hard disk two years ago and I suspect that you have profited from it to do the same with mine too.

>>> The girl who played with fire, p. 377

He bristled a bit, then named the document To Sally. So he created a folder, Lisbeth Salander, and put it in view on the desktop of his iBook.

>>> The girl who played with fire, p. 378

Interesting, isn't it? For a hacker it is a great show of confidence to respond to a message like that, because doing it implicitly reveals having access to your computer and being able to read and view all of your secrets.

Mikael returned home at one in the morning. He was tired and toyed with the idea of to hell with everybody and going to bed. But he turned on his iBook and checked his email. Nothing interesting came.
Then he opened Lisbeth Salander and discovered a new document. It was named To MikBlom and it was alongside the one he named To Sally. It was almost a shock to see it. She is here. Lisbeth Salander broke into my computer. Perhaps she is online right now. He double-clicked.

>>> The girl who played with fire, p. 409-410

However, because you never know in life, the hacker will have taken care not to leave any trace of his break-in.

He opened the information on the file and observed that the text was created less than fifteen minutes earlier. He suddenly smiled. The author was Mikael Blomkvist, Lisbeth had created it in his own computer and his own program. It was better than email, it left no traces ...

>>> The girl who played with fire, p. 410

Is it possible to realize that you are in the sights of a hacker who has already infected your computer? It is difficult, but not impossible. Start being suspicious if your PC starts to behave strangely or at times is very slow or if the light indicating hard disk activity is permanently on.
One suggestion is to not keep on your personal or company computer anything truly confidential, and even less so compromising, but use an external support to hook up only when you are not connected to the Internet.
However, if you have really angered a hacker, all your precautions will only serve to delay the inevitable.

YOUR WORST NIGHTMARE

They say that you can fear only what you at least partially know. Well, here is something else to fear.

If a hacker really wants to ruin you, but, like Lisbeth and her partners, is not lucky enough to find proof of any of your illicit acts using "traditional" methods, then some that you don't even imagine could happen.

What follows could happen even if the hacker has not infected your computer with a Trojan Horse, but let's assume that, like Lisbeth, he had done it with a program like Asphyxia, and let's say that he is really, really angry with you.

Having infected the computer, the hacker not only has access to all your information and can monitor in real time all your activities, including the typing in of passwords and mouse movements, he can also even access the internet using your PC as a source and run your email to all effects. Thus he can create email accounts, write on forums and write emails as if he were you, and even navigate and store information on your hard disk.

Let's say that he really wants to punish you, so he creates an email address that gives out information on an illegal child-pornography forum. Then he puts in your navigation cache pages and images of child-pornography sites, and downloads entire albums of illicit pictures on your computer, storing them in the hard disk so that not even you will ever be able to find them, perhaps protecting them with passwords. Then, to make the situation even worse, he will send emails to, or download pictures from, pedophile material exchange sites and so on. Then, after a week or month of activity like that, he can easily delete any trace of his presence on your PC, including the Trojan Horse, and wait for the police to do its work. The hacker knows that many child-pornography sites, as well as terrorism sites, are decoy sites created by law enforcement in various countries to identify those involved in this type of material.

A good mix of decoy sites and original addresses ensures the hacker that you will be involved in one of the many ongoing investigations: sooner or later you will receive a night visit from a special squadron and you will wind up in prison on one of the most notorious charges that exist: possession and distribution of child-pornographic material. Perhaps after a year of hell you will be able to demonstrate that you were victim of an elaborate scheme, but in the meantime the media will have destroyed you, you will have lost all your friends, and you will struggle to resume a normal life.

Child pornography is only one extreme example of illicit behavior that could be attributed to you if you are in the sights of someone able enough and angry enough. But the same goes for crimes that only require information system proof.

There are companies that specialize in developing "legal" Trojan Horses, i.e. available only to law enforcement, that are invisible to anti-virus programs. However, who can guarantee you that the distribution of these programs is perfectly under control and not used by private individuals to do something tremendous as we have just described?

This shows that for as prudent as you may be in never using a personal or company computer to store your secrets, there are still ways to deliberately create terrible and incriminating ones, even if very untypical of your behavior.

ATTACKS ON COMPANIES

...she had gone home and had turned on her Power-Book. It took her ten minutes to break into the Nobel agency's in-house network with the help of the password that she had memorized by casually observing the woman behind the counter which she typed in before uploading the pictures. It took her around three minutes to realize that fact that the computer that the woman was working on was also the company server – how stupid can someone be? - and another three minutes to gain access to all fourteen computers that comprised the network. After around two hours, she filtered Joakim Persson's accounting and observed that in the past two years he had evaded taxes on around SEK 750,000 in undeclared revenues. She downloaded all the necessary files and sent them to various internal revenues offices from a server address in the United States.

>>> The girl who played with fire, p. 97

Here is a classical demonstration that a hacker's activity is not limited to sophisticated attempts at attacking a computer or a network, but, more often than you think, at observing and exploiting human error.

As Lisbeth emphasized, letting employees work directly on its main server is one of the stupidest things that a company can do. An error by one person can automatically have an impact on the entire organization, even more than what would be possible if an individual were connected only to his own computer.

Naturally the fact that Lisbeth had found the company chief's undeclared accounting in plain site is a real stroke of fortune and further demonstration of the idiocy of the people in question. Let's not forget, however, that even if he were to find nothing, the hacker would easily be able to plant his own document demonstrating some hidden undeclared accounting that, as such, needs no other supporting evidence than the document itself.

Try to demonstrate the contrary after a regular audit by the authorities. As with child pornography, perhaps you could eventually, but in the meantime your entire business could go up in smokes.

Let's see now a more general feature of the vulnerabilities of a company organization.

After breaking into the network, a group of hackers can try to obtain as many credentials (usernames and passwords) as possible to then access it like any employee. They will focus on the credentials of the system administrators who, notoriously, can do anything, like access email and other users' files. This is certainly a key figure and, by pure chance, many system administrators even have a double life as a hacker, you can't imagine how many. Who could forget the scandal at the Liechtenstein central bank? The bank paid an information system consultant to manage information system security. Once inside, he copied everything on DVDs which he first used to blackmail the bank and a year later, he sold them to the German police for €2 million. You may wonder how it can be so easy, but always remember that your email and everything

that is managed by a company's network, for example your DSL connection, is in the hands of anonymous administrators who can do absolutely anything on that network.
Like I said, they can access your e-mail, see passwords (the best organized hackers directly copy the entire credentials databank) and, most of all, as administrators they do not leave the slightest trace. And when critical data are processed, such as databases containing telephone traffic or medical or bank transaction or credit card data, how hard do you think it is to copy daily on a DVD?
It may seem incredible, but system administrators almost never follow the security standards that apply, for example, for credentials. Instead they use generic usernames (admin, administrator, root, supervisor, etc.), normally with very weak passwords used by groups of people. It may seem like a shortcoming among administrators or negligence, but that's not the case. Systems with weak and generic supercredentials (i.e. non-nominal and usable by groups of people) ensure that the administrator can do whatever he wants without suffering any legal consequence for it in case of serious problems. So when you find a situation like this in a data processing center or in your IT division, you know that something is suspicious.

Around two in the afternoon she started up Asphyxia 1.3, but rather than MikBlom/laptop she selected MikBlom/office, Mikael's PC at the Millennium editorial office. She knew by experience that the computer that Mikael had in the office contained nothing interesting. He used it to surf the internet, but to work he had his iBook. Mikael was the administrator of Millennium's in-house network, so Lisbeth got his password.
To break into the other editorial office computers, however, the hard disk copied on the Netherlands server was not enough: the MikBlom/office original had to be accessed and connected to the in-house network. But lucky her. Mikael Blomkvist was at work and he had his computer on. Lisbeth waited ten minutes but saw no sign

of activity. Perhaps Mikael turned on the computer when he arrived at the office, but left it on idle while doing other things or working on his laptop.

>>> The girl who played with fire, p. 225-226

This is what happens when a hacker identifies a system administrator and manages to copy his credentials. Companies should be very careful, because the hacker could carry out all his controversial online operations through their computers and, with so many administrator credentials, he will more easily be able to consolidate his takeover and delete any trace.
Perhaps he will be satisfied with using your internet access to navigate anonymously. But if he engages in illicit operations, in case of serious problems you will be the one who pays for it.

IDENTITY THEFT

It is fair to say that the "identity theft" problem is one of the biggest side effects of the digital era and it is and always will be one of the greatest plagues of this century. Before Internet and computers, a person's identity was stored and certified by pieces of paper and it was not easy to get a hold of and use someone's identity, except for exotic disguises like in James Bond movies. Internet changed everything. To make it easy to use increasingly sophisticated technological and virtual services, our identities have been replicated in Cyberworld and, as time goes by, someone's cyber-identity gains more credibility than his real one. Will the day come when not being anyone in the virtual world will mean being no one in the real world?

This is indeed the trend. Conspiracy theorists say that this trend is part of a comprehensive control strategy whose aim is to create a soft global dictatorship. Perhaps a few years ago we would have laughed out loud, but now ... ?

As we have seen, computers and the human beings who use them are wells of vulnerability that are all transferred to our identity, if it is electronic.

More than twenty years ago, when in Europe there were still national borders and the first true hacker had not yet appeared,

I had a chance to meet a Dutchman who said that he could destroy any individual by inputting false information into the Interpol database. In other words, he claimed that he had a contact inside the Interpol information system division through whom he could input into anyone's file specific information such as "organ traffic" and similar: the next time that person crossed a border or police control, he would be arrested. If this happened in border countries, he could disappear forever.
But how is it possible, you may ask.
Well, it is possible only if, by convention, what a computer says is taken for truth.
If this was doable when there were only big mainframes used exclusively by big institutions, there is real reason to fear the thought of what could happen today, since everything which defines us as citizens is contained on one computer.
Lisbeth knows the power of identities and that machines recognize only virtual ones. As she is a true hacker, how could she not profit from it?
Thus in the second novel, Stieg Larsson has fun in constructing a bizarre and ironic situation during Lisbeth's research in judicial police files: a conflict of virtual identities.

To get into the records, she used the identity of commissioner Douglas Skiöld, 55 years old, serving the Malmo police district. It was a small shock when all of a sudden her computer made a beeping sound and a menu icon began to flash, signaling that someone was looking for her on the ICQ program.
She hesitated a second. Her first impulse was to pull the plug and disconnect. But she thought about it. Skiöld could not have an ICQ on his computer. Few people of his age had it, mostly young people and those who wanted to chat used it.
The meant that someone was looking for her. So she did not have many alternatives to choose from. She went on ICQ.

What do you want Plague?
Wasp. It's hard to find you. Don't you ever check your email?
How did you do it?
Skiöld. I have the list too. I supposed that you would have used one of the identities with several authorizations.

>>> The girl who played with fire, p. 489-490

Impressive, right? Two hackers collected identities of people in useful positions and communicate to each other through one of these which by chance they had both stolen. And that of a police commissioner.
Imagine two ventriloquists talking to each other using the same wooden puppet. What is impossible in the real world becomes possible in the Cyberworld.
How can this happen?
The explanation provided in the novel is entirely plausible and allows us to explain another aspect of hacking.
As a matter of fact, the first intrusion attempt into the police databank goes back a long time ago before the events narrated, and it happened without any specific reason. Nothing strange. Often a hacker is committed to penetrating a system as a simple "challenge" (personal or in competition with others) or to gather information that can be useful in some way in the future, for the pirate himself or for someone willing to pay.
Information systems, and the databases they contain, are very often handled by specialized outside companies whose technicians at times work there on a temporary basis. Hence internal network design, installation of all the computers, and, most of all, their administration and ordinary maintenance throughout almost the entire world are often in the hands of "civilians". This is how information that should be of strictest confidence and systems that should be managed with high level security procedures wind up in the hands of potential, fearful predators.
If one of these people is a hacker, do you think he can resist

the temptation in front of him? Lisbeth certainly did not resist, even for an obvious question of principle. Nonetheless, even an exceptional professional may come up against real difficulties.

The internal network was skillfully built, with its own cabling and shielding from outside connections and Internet. In other words, she needed a cop in flesh and blood with authorized access to the network helping her or the internal network had to believe that she was an authorized person.

>>> The girl who played with fire, p. 481

In Sweden, probably, security procedures are taken very seriously, so much so that even Lisbeth ran up against a concrete wall. What to do, then? All information systems have users with varying clearance levels to access information. So, in the absence of system vulnerabilities, the most logical alternative is to evaluate the famous human vulnerabilities, in other words those arising from idiocy, and then, once the first identity allowing system recognition is stolen, completely own it.

In that regard, luckily for her, police security experts had left a gigantic fault. Around the country a large number of police stations were hooked up to the network, many of small local units which were unguarded at night and in general had no alarm or surveillance system.

>>> The girl who played with fire, p. 481

You must know that the more a system is extended and spread over a vast territory, the more vulnerable it is, because the possibility that each access point is equally secure is almost zero. We have also seen that a chain is only as strong as its weakest link and this is also true for an information system

network. Since each individual computer in it (and each individual who uses it) is also indirectly connected to the system's core, why make life difficult and try to directly take over Fort Knox?
Take a look at how one person's idiocy can nullify the efforts of many to make a perimeter secure:

In around five minutes she found the username and password under the blotter on the commissioner's desk, and in one night of attempts she understood how the network functioned, identified the access code, and checked the security level. As a bonus she even obtained the username and password of two local agents.

>>> The girl who played with fire, p. 481-482

Ask yourselves how many people keep their username and password on a post-it stuck to their computer, in a drawer, or under the desk blotter. Take it easy, I won't ask you embarrassing questions.
Having credentials of two agents, for the network, is tantamount to having stolen their identities and the computer will give you access to its secrets just like it would do with them.

One of them was 31 year-old Maria Ottosson in whose computer Lisbeth found information on the fact that she had sought and obtained an investigator's job with the Stockholm police fraud unit. She was an easy target for Lisbeth because she had left her laptop in an unlocked drawer of the desk.

>>> The girl who played with fire, p. 482

Lisbeth was even luckier and she came across the identity of a person for whom security is a royal pain in the ass, thus putting at risk the entire team and its structure. Remember what we said about computers left unguarded. But there's worse:

Maria Ottosson was a policewoman with a private PC that she used at work. Wonderful. Lisbeth started up the computer and inserted a CD with Asphyxia 1.0, the very first version of her spyware program, which she installed as an integrated active part in Microsoft Explorer and as a back-up in the police address book. She figured that even if Maria Ottosson were to buy a new computer, she should have recovered her address book and there was a very good chance that she would transfer it to the computer at her new job with the Stockholm police fraud unit taking service there.

>>> The girl who played with fire, p. 482

If a person is allowed to use his or her personal computer to access a network, according to the weak link principle, the entire network will be just as vulnerable. Moreover, the personal computer will never be subject to the periodic scans that the network does of its content, thus also avoiding recognition of any viruses or Trojan Horses. Lisbeth also found a perfect way to achieve the longest takeover possible, as she had identified in the agent's personal address book the object that she would have certainly transferred to another computer.
Someone may ask: how can Lisbeth get to know the police system's internal control procedures so well? As she had access to systems and documents that described them on behalf of her employer, she learned exactly what to do to remain invisible in the network.

Plague scored a big success when he managed to break into the home computer of the police security division chief. He was a civilian without particular personal information system knowledge, with a large quantity of information in his laptop. With that, Lisbeth and Plague

would have a chance, if not to penetrate, at least to completely destroy the police information system network with harmful viruses of various kinds, something that neither one of them had the slightest interest in doing: they were hackers, not saboteurs. They wanted access to functioning networks, not to destroy them.

>>> The girl who played with fire, p. 483

It is hard but not impossible to find a network like the one described, i.e. with such efficient security technology as to prevent a total takeover, but this hardly matters when there are hundreds of identities available to access it. As you see, it is through an outside person who, in this case, holds a very important position like information system security chief, that Lisbeth and her partners managed to acquire the power to even destroy the police network. Power that they have intention of exploiting in "times of peace", but if the circumstances were to require it, who can say?
Already today our cyber-identity is used to identify us for banking, postal, telephone, and tax services, and increasingly for other public administration functions. To date, there is no single identity management system that is exempt from vulnerability, both technical and human. What would happen if one day a transfer came out of your bank account that left you out on the street? Or if your police file were embellished with something exotic and horrifying? Or if a telephone printout unmistakably said that we have frequent contact with a mafia boss?
The day that the entire sum of information that identifies us in society is managed by machines, how difficult will it be to fully delete a person with a click and thus in an instant take away all his rights as a citizen?

HACKERS WORKING FOR GOVERNMENTS

Would Lisbeth and her fellow citizens at Hacker Republic ever work for a government or institution?
Really, thinking of a hacker loyal to an establishment is like thinking of an anarchist recruited by the police force. Do not misunderstand me. I'm not saying that an anarchist would never let himself be recruited by a police force, but he certainly wouldn't do it for any "sense of country", rather to simply profit from the advantages of being inside the enemy fortress.
As we have seen, the true hacker starts with the desire to uncover any and all defects in the technology that, in his view, are the result of gross negligence by software producers, or have been introduced on purpose to allow any entity not known to us, such as the secret services of the various industrialized countries, to spy on and intercept communications as they see fit. Some countries with a high concentration of software technology producers, such as the United States, have established iron-clad rules on all industries seeking a license or to expand abroad. For example, if a cryptography program is impenetrable, it cannot be exported.

However, any software you buy, including ones included in a single package along with the computer, is marketed as the best and you pay a premium for it.

It is easy, then, to find hackers in environments at the borderline of subversion or where they can expose the games played by multinationals and the establishment that surrounds them. Among these hackers, it is easy to find those at the service of terrorism and organizations close to it: not by chance, in 2000 Osama bin Laden published the first manifesto on cyber-terrorism, a document called Al-jihad al-electronic. But even a hacker evolves over time, especially when he discovers the power that he wields over a network, keeping to himself the vulnerabilities that he has found for a long enough period to exploit them for his own advantage. Someone has discovered that there is an information market willing to pay a lot for a professional hacker's services. This market includes multinationals, especially drug companies, the information services of many countries and, last but not least, organized crime.

In the past few years, the international media has focused a lot of attention on how the United States or South Korea or India are setting up government hacker units. Well, it is easy to act from high up in an organization that in theory has all the access keys to the vulnerabilities of a technology that is sold to the public and without the scarecrow of being accused of a crime. However, remember that a true hacker will never be loyal to the establishment and if he does work for you, he does it only to get a hold of the "enemy's" secrets.

ORGANIZED CRIME: THE RUSSIAN BUSINESS NETWORK (RBN)

Since there has been an Internet, there have been hackers. In the beginning, however, the world's legislative systems hardly took the Internet and computers into consideration. For around a decade, hackers were able to act almost undisturbed and their exploits were told and exaggerated as myths by the media and in so many hardly realistic movies. After a long series of incidents on the Internet and when the various legal systems began to face big problems in the intent to prosecute hacker acts as criminal, then laws began to proliferate, starting obviously in the United States and Commonwealth countries, where the Internet started and where it began to spread the most, then a few years later also in Europe and finally in Italy.

Today any violation on the Web is punished very severely, almost as if it were armed robbery, rape, or even certain types of homicide, and increasingly they are reported in the headlines. This is the case in most countries, except in Russia, for example. Apparently, there the criminal code does not even define information system crime and this has favored the proliferation of innumerable forms of hackers and has facilitated the setting up of organizations whose only mission is hacking.

And Lisbeth does not even want to hear the names of such organizations and even she would stay away from them. But be clear: not because they are better than she is, but because what they do transcends all ethics, bordering on actual crimes against humanity.
The Russian Business Network is one of the most tentacled, efficient, and dangerous criminal organizations of all time. Here is the Wikipedia definition:

The Russian Business Network (RBN) is a multi-faceted cybercrime organization, specializing in and in some cases monopolizing personal identity theft for resale.

[...] RBN, which is notorious for its hosting of illegal and dubious businesses, originated as an Internet service provider (ISP) for child pornography, phishing, spam, and malware distribution. It is based in St. Petersburg. By 2007, it developed partner and affiliate marketing techniques in many countries to provide a method for organized crime to target victims internationally.

RBN has been described .... as the "baddest of the bad". It offers web hosting services and Internet access to all kinds of criminal and objectionable activities, with individual businesses earning up to $150 million in one year.

It sell its Denial of Service attack services to these businesses for $600 per month. The business is difficult to trace. It is not a registered company, and its domains are registered to anonymous addresses. Its owners are known only by nicknames. It does not advertise, and trades only in untraceable electronic transactions.

One increasingly known activity of the RBN is delivery of exploits through fake anti-spyware and anti-malware, for the purposes of PC hijacking and personal identity theft. In 2007, the information system threat matrix developed by Spy-Ops was ranked fourth in the development and sale of information system weapons.
[.]

RBN does business under several false names. Its operations apparently do not have a geographic base.
RBnet,
RBnetwork,
RBusinessnetwork,
iFrame Cash,
SBT Telecom network (Seychelles),
Aki Mon Telecom,
4Stat,
Eexhost,
DefconHost,
Rusouvenirs Ltd.,
TcS network (Panama),
Nevcon Ltd. (Panama),
Micronnet Ltd. (Saint Petersburg, Russia),
Too coin Software (UK),
76service,
MalwareRlarm (Czech Republic),
InstallsCash
[.]

It is believed that there are also presumed ties with the founder and head of the Flyman organization, which in turn has ties to a powerful and well known Russian political party.

In light of this, it is entirely possible that recent cyber-terrorism activities, such as the denial of service attacks on Estonia in May 2007 and Georgia and Azerbaijan in August 2008, may have been co-coordinated by or outsourced to such an organization. Although this is currently unproven, (US) intelligence estimates suggest this may be the case.

Doesn't this seem to you almost a description of the devil?
Well, rest assured that this is a very limited definition compared to what this organization really is. First of all, it does not only do business on the Internet. Internet serves as support, easily allowing all the criminal activities attributed to it

to take place in a totally asymmetrical way with respect to the countries around the world and to effortlessly reach any individual or any company that it wants to involve or strike.

Perhaps cyber-terror and cyber-war do not matter to the average citizen because they are very abstract prospects, which have little influence on our lives - apparently obviously.

However, the Russian Business Network's main mission is to develop its business and, of course, enormous quantities of money.

In order to do that, it operates on a vast scale to seize all the information that comprises our identity, and with that information also the tools that we use to, for example, make purchases, such as credit cards and deposit accounts.

But that's not all. It is believed that RBN also distributes extreme child-pornography material, including torture and even mutilations to the point of actual homicide, and it sells on the black market all kinds of illicit "merchandise", including human organs.

Naturally the Russian Business Network is only a sensational example, but similar organizations exist in support of all organized crime.

BECOMING A TARGET

The hacker organizations that are truly dangerous for everybody, and not only for governments or companies, are exactly those like the Russian Business Network that, from the heights of their position unassailable by laws and international regulations, see every single junction and computer on the network as a potential resource. Naturally they think big and they do not think of each individual in particular in their vast-scale operations.

When they succeed in infecting and possessing a computer, they do not want to damage it, on the contrary. They have the virus explore it for interesting information such as credit card numbers, usernames and passwords, complete personal data and so forth, then the same virus normally installs a tool that remains dormant and transforms the PC into what is known as a "zombie". A zombie computer can be re-awoken by a special signal, then it will be at the service of its “master”, doing exactly what is asked of it.

What makes us become a target?

It begins by being one of the masses sounded by criminal organizations as soon as they manage to get their hands on an

email address. How many times have you input your email address in one of those nice little fields in sites that say it is mandatory to register for the service offered? Think twice and be careful about giving it out because many of these sites periodically send to third parties their entire databank of addresses that they have gathered, and often the buyers are in fact criminal organizations. There are also fun softwares that scan the Internet in search of all websites, memorizing the email addresses of employees, customers, visitors, and in that case too you become a target, but with a major difference: the organization will have only an email address to work on, but no personal data.
One of the people close to Lisbeth, probably because of her work, gave out her email address once too often and here's what happens to her everyday:

Erika breathed, she connected her laptop, and she checked her email. She had 19 new messages. Four were spam from some who wanted 1) her to buy Viagra, 2) to offer her cybersex with the sexiest Lolitas on the net at a cost of only four USD per minute, 3) offer her the hottest animal sex, the juiciest horse fuck in the universe, and finally, 4) offer her a subscription to the mode.nu newsletter from a company that flooded the market with advertisements and never stopped sending its junk regardless of how many times someone expressly unsubscribes. Another seven were "Nigerian letters" from the widow of the former central bank governor of Abu Dhabi offering her fantastic sums if she would only contribute with a small amount of confidence money and similar ruses.

>>> The girl who kicked the hornet's nest, p. 365

How many people are targeted daily by this type of email? It is called spam, widespread emails that the user does not want and has not requested. Believe me, once you have gotten into this

circuit, you can never get out. Even if you ignore it, these emails will continue to come from apparently always different e-mail accounts and, if you make the mistake of opening one by mistake, then you are really ruined. Every one of these messages contains at least an image or a reference to a web page, even if you do not see it. Through the reference to an outside link, your computer makes a connection with the remote address that contains the image or the page. That's how, in an instant, the organization knows that you really exist and, most of all, that you open and read emails. Immediately your email address changes classification and is put in a more important databank: active email addresses.
Naturally something worse could happen, like as soon as your computer is connected to the spammer's remote address, the spammer downloads a code that exploits one of the many vulnerabilities of the software active on your computer and directly infects it. You may think that you have just opened an email, perhaps bothersome, and you will go on to something else, but by now you have been "possessed".
But that's not all. Some of these emails, the most insidious ones because they even seem legitimate, contain a warning that, if you do not want to receive that type of correspondence, asks you to write to a certain email address or click on a link. You respond or click and you are ruined.
Emails with these features not only have references to pharmaceutical drugs or pornography. At times they seem to be job offers, bank correspondence, travel agencies, and similar. Be aware of them all and, if you can, do not open them.
How can you protect yourselves? Avoid visiting strange sites, especially pornographic ones (a big blow, right?) because those are precisely the ones used by these kinds of organizations and, in many cases, just clicking on a link to a site can infect you. Do not respond to emails asking you for your credentials or data about you even if it really seems to come from your bank or some other known entity. Even better, do not open these emails at all!

One of the latest tricks used by big hacker organizations on the dark side occurred in 2009: a site inviting people to download a program giving access to many gigabytes of storage where you can store child pornography provided by the site itself. Well, the program that you are invited to download free of charge contains a Trojan Horse hidden in a jpg image. Download it and your computer will be at the service of these people.
Do you think that all those people who download it will file a claim that they have been infected in the attempt to download images that are borderline pedophile?.

THE NIGERIAN CLAN

Carefully reread this sentence:

Another seven were "Nigerian letters" from the widow of the former central bank governor of Abu Dhabi offering her fantastic sums if she would only contribute with a small amount of confidence money and similar ruses.

>>> The girl who kicked the hornet's nest, p. 365

Lisbeth is intimately familiar with the "Nigerian letters" chain. Do not be confused: it is obvious that this is a "chain" because almost everyone knows that Abu Dhabi is the capital of the United Arab Emirates which is on another continent and several thousand miles from Nigeria.
In the so-called underground where not only Lisbeth hangs around, but also those who, inside and outside the institutions, has fought against fraud, they say that Nigerians come into the world with an interesting and peculiar feature: the swindle and fraud gene. Never has anyone before them raised fraud to an international business and even today other organizations struggle to debunk the myth. We have to go back to a time

when computers were big closets and Internet was only a buzzword in someone's mind and in the speeches of a famous UC Berkeley researcher, between a beer and a joint: the legendary 1970s.
In the 1970s-1980s, a high number of people throughout the world received apparently important letters, elegantly type-written on paper with an institutional logo of the Nigerian government. The recipients were not just anybody, but selected individuals working in companies of all sizes or in top management or positions close to the finance and administrative departments of their firms. Here's an example of one:

Lagos, Nigeria.

Attention: The President/CEO Dear Sir,

Confidential Business Proposal

Having consulted with my colleagues and based on the information gathered from the Nigerian Chambers of Commerce And Industry, I have the privilege to request your assistance to transfer the sum of $47,500,000.00 (forty seven million, five hundred thousand United States dollars) into your accounts. The above sum resulted from an over-invoiced contract, executed, commissioned and paid for about five years (5) ago by a foreign contractor. This action was however intentional and since then the fund has been in a suspense account at The Central Bank of Nigeria Apex Bank. We are now ready to transfer the fund overseas and that is where you come in. It is important to inform you that as civil servants, we are forbidden to operate a foreign account; that is why we require your assistance. The total sum will be shared as follows: 70% for us, 25% for you and 5% for local and international expenses incidental to the transfer.
The transfer is risk free on both sides. I am an accountant

with the Nigerian National Petroleum Corporation (NNPC). If you find this proposal acceptable, we shall require the following documents:
your banker's name, telephone, account and fax numbers.
your private telephone and fax numbers —for confidentiality and easy communication.
your letter-headed paper stamped and signed. Alternatively we will furnish you with the text of what to type into your letter-headed paper, along with a breakdown explaining, comprehensively what we require of you. The business will take us thirty (30) working days to accomplish.

Please reply urgently.

Best regards

Howgul Abul Arhu

These letters were almost all the same, apparently written by a Nigerian government official, a minister for example, who magically had an exorbitant sum of money ($20-100 million) available but, unfortunately, for various reasons, it was impossible for him to transfer it abroad. The letter continued, asking help from the innocent and unaware recipient, convincing him that the favor asked was nothing in comparison to the potential benefit: the official offered a huge slice of his fortune. What did he want in return? Name and company position, authorized bank signature, letter-head, deposit account number, all fax numbers recognized by the bank, etc.
This was the first industrial-scale identity theft. Once they obtained this data, the Nigerians proceeded to empty the company's deposit account. In some cases the recipients were so greedy it led to idiocy: they did not provide their company's data, but their personal account data, causing a problem for the Nigerians who had to be satisfied with just a little.

Obviously many people just threw these letters away, but the Nigerians acted according to a statistical method: out of a thousand attempts, there had to be at least one imbecile. The same person was the target of such a letter at least once a year, using the old tactic of the door-to-door salesman who will come the day that somebody, for one reason or another, has his defenses down and instead of slamming the door in his face let's him enter.

With the advent of the Internet, the Nigerian chain letter went viral, multiplying and accelerating exponentially. Now, instead of letters, people receive emails which have the same features of spam as described above and, if opened, could transfer an undesired code into the computer.

Today these messages no longer seem to come from Nigerian officials, but from Arabs, Asians, etc., enough to dodge all filtering systems that, upon detecting the word "Nigeria", automatically trash the letter. The content is always the same, but, do not be deceived then, it is always them.

HACKER COALITIONS

According to myth, there really were vampires on Earth, like many other strange, fantastic or terrible races. They say that vampires were formidable warriors and, though not immortal like the novels suggest, they lived a really long time, they were powerful lone wolves, and most of them lived at the margins of human society, making contact only to feed themselves. But the most interesting feature is their aggressiveness against their own kind.

If there is truth to the myth, in terms of psychology and character, hackers could be considered one of the possible evolutions of the vampire race: lone wolves, detached, night owls, fond of hidden places, extremely individualistic, manipulators, making human contact only to satisfy their own fundamental needs, and above all they live in a constant state of cold war with everyone of their own kind, especially when on the Internet. The malice that a hacker can demonstrate towards another hacker on the Internet can be compared only to the homicidal fury of a vampire against another vampire, while in so-called hack meetings, which are held several times a year in different places throughout the world, they meet as if in a demilitarized zone. More than anything else, what unchains a hacker's fury against another is if one says that he is or, if in one way or another, seems to be better than the rest.

Kevin Mitnick's story

A sensational example is one of the first hackers who became world famous in the 1990s, Kevin Mitnick. After doing his time in a federal prison, Kevin opened a security protection business, affirming that his site was impenetrable. Well, two days later a complete copy of all Kevin's and his company's material and email was going around on the Internet.

And this was repeated in 2009 just before one of the most famous and attended hackers conferences in the world: DefCon in Las Vegas. Kevin was persecuted up to that event where he publicly complained because his Internet service provider and the US telephone company AT&T informed him that he was an undesirable customer because of the unending number of attacks that their networks were suffering because of him.

Nonetheless, strangely there are times and situations when hackers join forces against a common target and when it happens among Lisbeth and her fellow citizens of Hacker Republic it works like a charm.

Normally the community reacts against the "system" by displaying an outstanding anarchical tendency and uncommon camaraderie when one of their members is attacked. If it does happen, whoever or whatever entity the target is, it'd better begin to tremble in view of the tremendous damage that could be done to people or technological structures.

To make an example that summarizes everything that has been written about Lisbeth, organizations like Hacker Republic and what motivates a hacker with the passion of a predator in a glade full of happy cows, I will mention an event that really took place.

A hacker known on the Internet as Neo (remember Matrix?) and part of an international hacker organization known as Team Elite penetrated and possessed the website of the UK's legendary MI5 secret intelligence service, installing a virus that could have infected the computer of any visitor. Fortunately, it seems that their purpose was only to find vulnerabilities and make them known.

CYBER STALKING

The image was pornographic. A naked woman with exceptionally well developed tits and a chain around her neck, on all fours, with someone penetrating her from behind.

But the woman's face was replaced, and not well made-up, probably intentional. The face of Erika was pasted to the original. The image was of her editorial in Millennium, it could have easily been downloaded from the Internet.

A word was written on the lower margin, using the Photoshop spray function:

Slut.

It was the ninth anonymous message received containing the word "slut", apparently coming from a big Swedish daily. She was in the clutches of a cyber stalker.

>>> The girl who kicked the hornet's nest, p. 472

Stalking means obsessive pursuit of a person. It is a rather frequent phenomenon and there are interesting criminological studies on it. Here is an abstract from the Wikipedia definition.

As suggested by the scientific literature on tormenting harassment, stalking means a series of continuous bothersome conduct, consisting of uninterrupted positioning near the victim's residence or places frequently attended, further reiterated with intrusions in the victim's private life in the attempt to make personal contact by means of shadowing and obscene or unwanted telephone calls. It also means the sending of letters, notes, e-mails, SMS, unrequested objects, or writings on walls or acts of vandalism damaging goods in a persistent and obsessive way, in a crescendo culminating in written and verbal threats, sometimes degenerating into physical aggression with injury to and even the killing of the victim. All the above, or part of it if done persistently and tenaciously so as to cause fear and psychological or physical unease by the victim, is stalking and the person who does it is a stalker. In some countries, stalking is a criminal act and the person who perpetrates can be punished by law. It is distinct from simple harassment by the frequency and duration of the various repeated types of behavior.
There have always been stalkers, but with technology they have invented many new ways of pursuing it, along with traditional methods.
In this case, an acquaintance of Lisbeth became the victim of a stalker who acted mainly through email and the Internet.
Some suggestions for those who feel they are being followed, and so a foreword: in Italy too stalking has become a crime, punishable with prison, and the first cases have already begun to appear in the media.
First of all, pursuit via text messages is a rather naive method because if something is easily traceable in the digital era it is the cell phone. By law, it is no longer possible to obtain anonymous SIM cards and, even if it were, the cell phone itself has a code that continuously transmits to the network, making it one of the least private forms of communication in the world. This code is called IMEI and, as we have seen, through it calls can be intercepted regardless of the SIM card used.
But please do not mistake a person who overwhelms you with

text messages for a stalker. A stalker, whether or not you know him, is threatening in his communications: his purpose is to hunt you down and cause deep fear, and he knows that he could be prosecuted. If he wants to text you, he will do it through a public telephone or a website that allows the sending of text messages to cell phones.

Whether he uses a public telephone or the Internet, in most cases you will note that a strange number appears in the sender field. This number should identify the service and its provider. But since there is no public directory for these codes, the only way to trace it to the sender is to file a complaint, but that would be almost useless: in the case of a public telephone, you would have to not only identify it, but catch the person in the act. And it is even more complicated with the Internet because, if not completely stupid, the stalker will tend to use a service based abroad. So, in order to have a slight chance of tracing it to the original computer, an investigator would need to send an international rogatory letter. And, in 99% of the cases, the answer is that data are no longer available. Remember that Internet is a world unto itself, with its attributes, the most important of which is the total absence of borders and jurisdictions.

Obviously these limits apply to a country's police forces which are bound by laws and regulations. Everything changes if you have a hacker friend who can help you. If motivated enough, the hacker would quickly trace the service that allows the stalker to ruin your life and, after studying its vulnerabilities, he would have a greater chance of gaining control of it in expectation of the next message. At that point, by identifying the IP address, he could attempt a direct connection with the computer from which the messages originate and trace the author. Alternatively, you could provide law enforcement with the IP address, but it would be hard for them to use if because it was acquired by "unconventional" means and so no prohibited by law.

If the stalker uses e-mail, everything changes. Every message, even when sent through anonymous addresses, perhaps

abroad, contains a section with registration data, which the user normally does not see. It often contains also the IP address of the originating computer and then it's game over.
Unless the person stalking you is a hacker (shame on all hackers) or simply a prudent person with better than average knowledge of information technology. In such case, he will connect via Wi-Fi services not traceable to him or, only to traumatize you, from a public place where he does not have to leave his name.
Here then is a trick that Lisbeth could suggest you use, always with the help of a hacker like her. Some methods that spammers use can be put at the service of the light side of the force: one of these tricks consists of preparing an e-mail from your address targeted by the stalker, perhaps responding to one of his messages, with a very small image included which is on a server available to your hacker friend, and then wait. A stalker will certainly open a message coming from his victim, and suddenly the small image will be downloaded and you will know his IP address. However, there is always the possibility that he opens your e-mail from a public address, so in this case too you will draw a blank. Unless your hacker friend is someone like Lisbeth and then ... she could include a small Trojan Horse in the image that gives her access to the stalker's computer. But be careful not to cross the line from right to wrong by exaggerating.
In her conviction that she is on side of right, Lisbeth did even worse in identifying the bad guy who was bothering her friend. Assuming that he was someone who knew her, probably from her new workplace, she obtained network access credentials and from there she copied and analyzed the content of everyone's e-mail until she traced the probable candidate stalker. Effective, yes, but unfortunately very borderline.

SECRET BASES IN CYBERWORLD

Since the year one, members of secret or underground organizations or associations have met in hidden places and their identities have been guarded with maximum reserve, often unknown even to their fellow members. However, in the physical world there must be at least someone who knows them all, otherwise it would be really difficult to have affiliations. In Cyberworld, this is no longer a constraint and the secrecy of members' identities can be easily guarded since it is not at all essential for the organization to know its members' activities in real life.

When a new member is selected, he is known only by his Internet identity and his hacker name, like Wasp, which is Lisbeth Salander's name. Only the member's value counts and this is measured by his gestures and exclusively by his peers, and it is always and only associated with his hacker name.

Every honorable secret association offers a hidden place where other members can talk and openly compare notes and where banned recipes come to life from the melting pot of their unconventional minds.

Hackers came into existence with the virtual big bang that generated Cyberworld and they immediately began to get

together in communities which were completely unbalanced with respect to the national conventions of the physical world. And then, since technology began to make it possible, they have set up refuges that exist in an alternative reality in Cyberworld.
Some secret intelligence services, even those not too friendly to Europe and the US, have imitated this model.
But let's first see how the organization called Hacker Republic behaves: Lisbeth is now trying to work a code that will give her access to the parallel world of her peers.

She began by visiting a private page that advertised boring pictures by an unknown, amateur and not particularly skilled photographer called Gill Bates from Jobsville, Pennsylvania. Lisbeth had once checked and observed that there is no town called Jobsville. Nonetheless, Bates had taken more than two hundred pictures of it and put them together in a photo gallery.

>>> The girl who kicked the hornet's nest, p. 381-382

Hackers are very proud of their sarcastic sense of humor. Of course Gill Bates is an anagram for Bill Gates, the founder of Microsoft, whom many hackers consider akin to the devil. And to say that he lives in Jobsville is a reference to Steve Jobs, one of the founders of Apple, Microsoft's and PCs' perennial rival.
Do not be deceived: Lisbeth is following a complex procedure that will lead her exactly to where she wants to go.

Lisbeth downloaded image number 167 and clicked on zoom. The photo represented the Jobsville church. She moved the cursor on to the bell tower steeple and clicked.

>>> The girl who kicked the hornet's nest, p. 382

Of course these and other complex procedures were put in place to prevent a casual Internet surfer from discovering that what he has found is, in fact, an access portal to a secret and parallel world. Though the access procedures are complicated and highly secure, merely discovering the portal would pose a big risk to the entire organization for various reasons, the most important of which is that it could be put under surveillance. And sooner or later someone particularly skilled would be able to steal the identity of one of the members and access their protected world.

Immediately a window opened that asked for identity and password. She took out her digital pen and wrote Remarkable in the identity field and A(89)Cx#Magnolia in the password field. A window popped up with the text Error you have the wrong password along with a box with Ok try again. Lisbeth knew that if she clicked on Ok try again and entered a new password the same window would appear again, no matter how many times she tried. Instead she clicked on the letter o in Error.

>>> The girl who kicked the hornet's nest, p. 382

This is how the credentials should be for anyone to access a system and prevent many people from being the victims of identity theft.

First, the username should always be an anonymous word or series of words, not referable to any name and certainly not connected to you in any way: the ideal situation is that only you know it.

The password must be complex and contain not only alphabetical and alphanumeric characters. Moreover, it should be longer than eight characters in order to make it very complicated for anyone trying to find it out with the help of password cracking programs and also to prevent anyone seeking your password and your preferences from guessing it. This procedure should lead you to the next level (not to direct access to the system), and only you and other members know that it works like this.

The screen turned black. Then an animated door opened and something that looked like Lara Croft came out. A comic strip materialized with the text Who goes there?

She clicked on the comic strip and wrote Wasp. She immediately saw the response Prove it or else ... while Lara Croft unlocked the safety on the gun. Lisbeth knew that the threat had some teeth. If she wrote the wrong password three times in a row, the page would turn off and the name Wasp would be deleted from the members list. She wrote the password MonkeyBusiness. The screen again changed look and a blue background appeared with the text:

Welcome to Hacker Republic, citizen Wasp. It is 56 days since your last visit. There are 10 citizens online. Do you want to 1) browse the forum 2) send a message...

>>> The girl who kicked the hornet's nest, p. 382

Once the identity of the person is checked for the last time, the system finally gives free access, which will of course also be encrypted, though this detail is not disclosed by Lisbeth.

These few lines truly summarize a real system access security procedure that blocks out would-be identity thieves and curious casual surfers.

One of the biggest faults of any system connected to the Internet – which is made clear also by how Lisbeth and Plague gained access to the Swedish police network – is precisely the documentation that describes it in fine detail.

With this documentation, a hacker has it on a silver platter because it allows him to know the system's exact responses to any stimulus and, most of all, it tells him precisely how serious the level of security applied is. For example, when a safecracker sees a new model, he immediately tries to obtain the documentation that describes it to learn what tools to use to break into it.

Many years ago, a carmaker put on the market a model of car that, it said, was theft-proof. To demonstrate it, the company hired two professional car thieves just out of prison and asked them to try to open the lock. The thieves observed the superb car and asked to have the instruction manual. They flipped through it casually and, after a few minutes, one of them scrutinized the front bumpers and landed a swift kick in a precise point. By miracle, the car opened. Astonished, the carmaker's representatives asked the thieves how they did it and they simply responded that there had to be a security mechanism to allow the passenger to get out in case of emergency and all that they had to do was locate the front collision sensor. Clear?

Whenever possible, never explain to anybody, for any reason, how the security system for something works, because knowing it means it is possible to break into it.

THE CRASH BANG JOB: HACKERS IN ACTION

HOLD PLEASE

From the moment telecommunications made it possible to eliminate distances there has been tapping and, of course, professional hackers know the secrets of it. Lisbeth is the first to have no qualms in doing it to solve her first mystery. Through her affiliation with Hacker Republic, she has access to one of the greatest experts in the area:

At five in the afternoon they were standing at the bar when they were approached by a man around 30 years old. He was almost bald, but had a blond beard, and he was wearing a jacket that was too big, jeans, and sailing shoes. "Wasp?", he asked.

"Trinity?", she replied. Both nodded. The man didn't ask what Mikael's name was.

Trinity's partner was introduced as Bob the Dog. They were waiting in an old Volkswagen van around the corner. They got in through the sliding doors and sat down on seats set to the walls. While Bob was weaving through London traffic, Wasp and Trinity were talking. "Plague said that this was a crash-bang job."

"Wire tapping and tracking email on a computer. It

could be very fast or it could take a couple of days, depending on how much pressure he will put." Lisbeth gestured her thumb towards Mikael. "Can you do it?"

"Child's play", responded Trinity.

>>> The Girl with the Dragon Tattoo, pp. 558-559

Now let's take one small step back. Our adventure begins with the death of Martin Vanger, the homicidal monster who was flushed out and cornered by Lisbeth's unconventional operations. Martin died in an accident trying to flee by car. However, the disappearance of Martin's sister Harriet is still a mystery. Lisbeth and Mikael Blomkvist are persuaded that she is not dead, but instead she fled from her brother Martin's homicidal fury with the help of her cousin and best friend Anita Vanger. The only information that Wasp and Mikael have is Anita Vanger's London address, and for Lisbeth this is enough.

And it's here that the Cyberworld works its miracles. Do you remember the old cop movies? In order to trace a phone call, the police had to trace a line and it took a few minutes to happen, making it necessary to keep the person on the phone for as long as possible. But in the era of digital communications, this is no longer necessary.

Every time we call someone, our telephone transmits a series of information on the network to the service provider and to the recipient. This is the case for all domestic calls, though there may be exceptions for international calls: when a call goes from the national telephone company to another country, one of them, for various reasons, could decide to cut the information and then, if you are the recipient of the call, the cell phone display could typically read "unknown caller". In this case, identifying where the call originated is really difficult.

But many people think that by instructing the phone (cell or landline) not to send their number, the phone actually carries out the order. Wrong.

Even when we want to stay anonymous, in fact our phone

always sends out our number to the network and the recipient, associating a tiny code that forces the receiving phone not to show the number. In this case we will see appearing on the display "unknown number" or "private caller", which means that there is a number, but the person calling does not want to reveal it. You know that there is a way to get around this procedure, though most of the time it is only possible by contacting the telephone company. Normally this "option" is granted only after filing a complaint with the authorities for serious issues, as in the case of stalking. The different telephone companies have different names for this kind of service, but in general is it known as “over-ride category". A suggestion for the privacy authority: this service could be granted as a “favor” to important people or those with good contacts in the telephone company even in the absence of a complaint, hence it would not be a bad idea if telephone company's check all users with this active service.

There are several cases in English-speaking countries where hackers like Trinity changed their telephone's software to show the caller's number in any case, but the hacker must be particularly skilled.

Let’s see now how Liz and her fellow citizens of Hacker Republic identify Harriet Vanger, who had disappeared from her family more than forty years ago, but most of all let’s clarify how come the police didn’t get there first. Well, first of all, for an operation like this, which involves several countries, it takes truly asymmetric action, in other words with an organization that operates without the hindrance of national rules and hands tied by agreements among police forces. Since the key person is located in London and not Sweden, and since Hacker Republic citizens do not recognize traditional borders, but only the non-existent ones of Cyberworld, their solution proves to be more effective.

In the hackers’ world it is unlikely that you’ll find a single individual expert in all technologies and every aspect of their vulnerabilities. There is a sort of unwritten cooperation agreement that is part of the hacker code and that can very

simply be summarized as "one hand washes the other" or "I do you a favor and you do me a favor", and, when that is not possible, an agreement is made for compensation in money. For example, the hacker who knows everything about Windows systems is not necessarily likewise skilled with Apple systems, or the hacker who knows everything about databanks does not necessarily know all the secrets of telecommunications, etc.
Trinity's skill in telecommunications is unrivaled, and Lisbeth knows it, while the origin of his genius traces the lines of development of any professional hacker worthy of the name:

He was thirty-two years old, born in Bradford, but he lived in northern London since he was a child. His education was rather poor, but he earned a certificate as telecommunications technician at a trade school. Starting at the age of nineteen, he worked for three years as an installer for British Telecom. But his skill in electronics and information systems allowed him to discuss these topics with any snob professor.

>>> The girl who kicked the hornet's nest, p. 449-450

Imagine Mozart going to piano school. He does it because he wants to know all the rules of the world where he is master by birth right, in addition to earning the degree to penetrate its secrets.

He had lived with computers since he was ten and he broke into one for the first time at thirteen. This whetted his appetite and when he was sixteen he was so good that he competed with the best hackers in the world.

>>> The girl who kicked the hornet's nest,, p. 450

We can easily say that all hackers go through a phase where they are not even aware of the consequences of certain actions.

So they experiment in every way and try to measure up to those who, like them, belong to Cyberworld. The sense of power they get from being able to break into any prohibited place is intoxicating and often even dangerous, if not lethal.

There was a time when he spent days in front of the screen every waking minute, putting together his own programs and setting insidious traps on the Internet. He nested inside the BBC, the UK Ministry of Defense, and Scotland Yard. He even managed, fleetingly, to take command of a UK atomic patrol submarine in the North Sea.

>>> The girl who kicked the hornet's nest,, p. 450

At this stage a sort of natural selection occurs, during which the hacker can choose to break through to the famous "dark side" and be dominated by it, or he can stay down to earth, without however giving up the chance to move in the dark folds of the Cyberworld and control its darkness.

Luckily Trinity was on the side of information system pirates who are more curious than evil. And his curiosity was satisfied as soon as he was able to break into a computer and take over its secrets.

>>> The girl who kicked the hornet's nest, p. 450

Another test that the hacker has to pass to cross the line and bring him to maturity is the test of vanity posed by the sensational aspects of his undertakings, often considered at the threshold of magic. Those who do not resist the temptation to let their gestures be known often wind up dead.
Kevin Mitnick's story
Let's take a real example: Kevin Mitnick, the world's most famous hacker who in the 1990s drove US federal law enforcement, especially the FBI, literally crazy, at times

completely unprepared to face an unknown threat of that size. Kevin's hacker name in Cyberworld was Condor, a name he chose after having seen the legendary movie with Robert Redford Three Days of the Condor. His raids began to cause him some problems in the very early stages of his development and in the 1980s it cost him several minor convictions.
However did not give up and he decided to totally embrace the "dark side". He posed a challenge to multinationals and the federal government by putting to work his intelligence, technical skill, ingenuity, and the stupidity of his adversaries through social engineering. He reached the core of government systems and managed to monitor every step taken by FBI investigators who were hunting him uselessly, until the final capitulation in 1995 after a 168-day manhunt without pause.
Kevin was put in prison without a trial in 2000 and then he had to undergo a period of forced abstinence from computers for three years before going back into action, but this time with the white hat of a security expert. The Condor paid a high price for his choice. Luckily not everyone follows his path.
Lisbeth knows that Trinity is one of those who have passed the test and that, in normal life, he uses his "powers" very judiciously:

He studied telecommunications technology because he already knew how the telephone network functioned, and after having observed that it was hopelessly obsolete he became a private consultant. He installed alarm systems and he monitored intrusion detection systems. For very special customers he could even offer refinements such as telephone monitoring and wire tapping.

>>> The girl who kicked the hornet's nest, p. 450-451

Now that it is clear what type of hacker is needed to work undisturbed on the telephone network, let's go back to how the disappeared Harriet is traced.

Wasp needs to tap Anita Vanger's telephone and Internet communications in the hope that the two come into contact. To achieve her objective, with Mikael's help, Wasp sets up a ingenious trap through a provocation.

These kinds of provocations are very similar to the ones that police use in the course of apprehending some criminal: he is distractedly left alone with an accomplice or relative in a room equipped with hidden microphones so that, blinded by panic and adrenaline, he says something fundamental. Or everyday someone "negligently" leaves a cell phone with him so that he can send messages, giving away accomplices that perhaps investigators are not yet aware of. At times even office or home searches are "staged" or only for the purpose of breaking the ice and observing how the target person behaves.

Wasp contrives something very similar: first she contacts Trinity, another hacker and fellow citizen of Hacker Republic, then she arranges the service, sending the victim's coordinates. Since this is not a cell number, Trinity prepares the tapping with a transmitter on the small tower (or on the closet) of the local landline and she waits in her van.

Once the preparation work is complete, Trinity and Wasp only have to wait for the trap to spring and so Mikael Blomkvist goes to Anita's house and says the magic words, leaving the bait. At that point, she picks up the phone and calls Harriet. In this case, since its an outgoing call, the telephone number dialed is obtained very simply from Anita's dialing and identified, and Harriet's identity is confirmed. In this case there was no need to eavesdrop on the conversation because the objective was merely tracing where the disappeared Harriet Vanger was located.

But don't think it has to do with magic. Locating a landline number is as easy as looking in the phone book or using the white pages service on the Internet.

But locating a cell phone is more sophisticated, because it requires at least having access to telephone network data that precisely indicates which antenna in the world the telephone is using to transmit. However, since cell phones are equipped with GPS antennas, through the IMEI code which unmistakably identifies them throughout the world, the cell phone can be contacted and precisely located to the millimeter through the GPS service. Hope that you are never in the sights of a guided missile

PAYMENTS AMONG HACKERS

If someone is really good, hacking is an occupation that can pay extremely well. Especially because what the hacker is being asked to do always smacks of being well "off limits" to come cheaply and Lisbeth is well aware of this. In the case of locating Harriet Vanger, Wasp arranged for Trinity to receive a money payment. There are many ways in which this transaction could take place between hackers. The two more immediate methods include cash, where hackers would obviously have to meet, as in this case. The alternative and more commonly used method is provided through a handy service available on the Internet, known as e-gold, or «electronic gold» (www.e-gold.com). Until quite recently, this was the method of choice for whoever carried out transactions that needed to be to kept secret. This is how it works: an account is opened on the service using a name (not subject to verification). Money is then transferred into the account by credit card or bank transfer, and is instantly transformed into virtual «gold», so that the money deposited is then subject to market fluctuations in the value of gold. But that's not all: this service also allows for transactions between people registered on the service. Basically, a registered user transfers an amount of virtual gold to another registered user, irrespective of where

that user may physically be located in the world. It's efficient, simple and above all, invisible.
Similarly, turning the virtual gold back into money is a very simple transaction: all that is required is the details of a current account or any money transfer service.
Not only hackers make use of this system. It is quite simple for organized crime or terrorist organizations to make their money disappear within the Cyberworld, and then make it reappear wherever they want.
Just think that this service - and many others, although much less significant - have been active since at least 1996.
Getting back to the way hackers collaborate, we can state quite categorically that the method of choice is not payment in money, but rather, as stated previously, an exchange of similar services. A sort of bartering system.
In the case of Wasp, for example, instead of agreeing on a money payment, Trinity would probably have asked Lisbeth for the telephone records relating to a series of Swedish numbers, which perhaps came off the Telenordia operator (that she was connected with). Many professional hackers use their «dead times» to conduct searches with the sole purpose of accumulating information and data banks that could prove useful at the appropriate time in their transactions with other hackers. Lisbeth had effectively accumulated a store of information worthy of the secret services, by infecting company and private computers that she considered of interest with Asphyxia, the Trojan Horse that she herself created, with instructions to forward all the data contained on the hard disk. The Swedish Police, the Judicial Archives and the Judge investigating her were all completely at her mercy.
We have seen how hackers use a sophisticated technique called «Social Engineering», which has nothing to do with the information side of things, to great advantage. They build up a network of people in key positions according to their needs, as for example, within a data processing center of a telephone operator, so as to be in a position to exchange «favors» when the need arises.

TAPPING: WHAT IS IT AND HOW IT IS DONE

The whole question of telephone and information tapping is quite widespread. Some people believe that they are always been listened in on or they fabricate incredible stories about something they actually know nothing about. In recent years, there has also been excessive talk on the subject in Parliament with the scandals regarding legal and illegal tapping on the increase, and reaching levels that remind of the TV show "The Twilight Zone". I once happened to hear a well-known political figure speaking on a TV show, and believe me, it was quite hilarious: «My phones are being tapped continuously» he stated. «Come on, how can you say that? » asked the curious TV host. «Often, when I'm in the middle of an important phone call, I hear noises and sometimes someone even coughing and do you know what I do? I say hello to the policeman on the other side. I've got nothing to hide!»
It makes you smile, doesn't it? Seems like something taken from an Italian comedy movie. So then according to this eminent politician, whoever is tapping the phone isn't just listening in and recording, but has added a microphone while he's at it, so that he can interact with the victim. I can just imagine him suggesting to the person being tapped to speak a little louder or closer to the receiver or to move somewhere

quieter.
It is worth taking time to dispel some of the «false myths» about tapping.
The first thing you should know is that if you're someone normal, with usual day-to-day activities and a clean record, and your greatest crime is putting together a carbonara without adding the bacon, well then, it's probably not worth the effort to tap your phone. But there is certainly someone among you «normal» readers that has heard (or used) a sentence similar to one of these: «Listen, let's speak face to face, because you never know…» «How come an unidentified number has come up? Something strange is going on…» Or else, in the country that gave birth to Divorce, Italian style: «But are you sure your husband isn't listening in on us?»
We really need to clear things up and reassure all the victims of urban legends that telephone tapping is not that simple.
The Judicial Authorities and the Police can tap a phone (land line or cellphone), but in order to do this, they need to have an order that has been proposed by a Prosecutor and authorized by an Investigating Judge which is then passed on to the telephone operator for a limited period of time (about fifteen days, and is renewable). In theory this only happens in relation to people that have committed quite serious crimes. The reasons for this are not only the privacy laws, but also the costs, which are significant.
Legally tapping someone's phone means setting in motion a huge operation. Starting with the Attorney General and the Judicial Police that need to allocate specific staff and adequate resources and technology, which are largely rented from private individuals. And ending with the telephone companies that are obliged by law («mandatory rendering of services») to make entire sections with many employees available, together with the technology and space required to conduct the operation. There has been a great deal of discussion on whether tapping serves a purpose. Whoever watches too many American movies would probably conclude that it is easy to catch a criminal by what he says on the phone: «So then we've

agreed! Take all the drugs to pier 4, I'll have the money ready, and the deal is done!» Or else: «Go and kill Pippo with a shot in the heart and one in the head… You'll find him down at the sports bar! » Or in the case of terrorists: «We need to strike a decisive blow against the current imperialist dictatorship! Activate the bomb!»

For the most part, criminals and terrorists lead quite normal lives, with most of their day dedicated to work, chatting with friends, seeing the dentist, their mom, girlfriend, and lover etcetera; and when they do have something specific to say, they probably don't discuss it on the telephone. A look at the statistics (if such statistics were to exist), as to how many phone taps actually succeed would give us a clearer idea.

It could happen that you unfortunately find yourself caught up in an investigation with your phone being tapped. It is very important then to keep something in mind: according to Italian Law whatever you say on the telephone constitutes proof of guilt and in cases where there is intense media pressure and therefore an urgent need to close off an investigation by finding someone guilty, you should pay close attention to what you say on the telephone. Hands up who has at least once said something like: «Bring the stuff with you», «I swear I could kill him! » «You remember that thing we wanted to do… Yes, that's right… Well, it's done! » «But isn't there some way we can avoid having all this money taken off us by the tax man? »

One day you could find yourselves in a position where you would have to explain similar utterances; after being arrested perhaps (also called «preventative custody»). Rest assured that in the darkness of your cell, you'll find yourselves ready to confess to anything, even the assassination of JFK or Roberto Calvi.

Don't be too alarmed. These are extreme cases. Freedom of speech and expression are sacred institutions when you find yourselves in a position where you have to explain what you said.

A word in the ear of those prone to boasting: be careful what you boast about on the phone.

If you are being tapped, anything you say can constitute an element of proof for any crime whatsoever. To get some kind of reaction, I once asked an eminent judge what would happen if a person who was being tapped admitted to working with the Martian Emperor to overthrow the democratic order on Earth. He replied that he would be considered a lunatic because it was not credible (aliens do no exist by law).
But if by some misfortune, you are being tapped and while chatting with a friend you throw in something like: «Tonight I'm going to rob a bank», intended as an exaggeration, when you actually meant that you were going to be withdrawing money from an ATM, well, that could be all it takes for the special forces to breakdown your door and take you away.

WHO CAN TAP AND HOW IT WORKS

As we have seen, the procedure involved is complicated for the telephone operator and involves so many people that someone acting individually could never tap in and remain unpunished for long. A well-publicized example involved Vodafone in Greece a few years ago, where secret service agents (never publicly disclosed) had the heads of the telephone network on their payroll, so they could intercept politicians and other leading figures. Shortly after being disclosed, the Director of the Company mysteriously committed suicide, and the matter was brushed under the carpet after a few articles were published in the newspapers. We are naturally referring to the secret service agents of a Country with the resources to be able to set up such a complex, delicate and costly structure. Needless to say we're not referring to the Greek secret service, but other foreign powers. Even in Italy, the telephone network provides a strategic information service and, in circumstances that threaten national security, it could be used by whoever is authorized to make use of it. Clearly, it is obvious that the secret services of another Country could never legally intercept calls in Italy.

With regard to the secret services, it is worth noting a few things about the Italian secret services in order to debunk a couple of other myths. Firstly, there is very little the secret services can do legally: for example, Italy is the only Country in the world where they cannot conduct any interceptions or tapping of any kind. Nor can they demand telephone records, unless this is done through the appropriate Judicial Police channels. The only thing they can do legally on Italian national soil is to pay experts, who then assume criminal responsibility for whatever they are doing. A rather strange procedure. While the tapping carried out by telephone operators in relation to mobiles and land lines is largely identical, there is a substantial difference when the relevant authorities are not involved, but it involves a private investigator or hacker.

MOBILE TAPPING

Let's take a look at how Trinity and Bob the Dog conduct themselves while working for Lisbeth.

The telephone tapping was a more difficult task than the computer monitoring. Trinity had no trouble locating the cable to Prosecutor Ekström's home telephone.
The problem was that Ekström seldom or never used it for work-related calls.

>>> The Girl who kicked the hornet's nest, p. 472 (325)

With the advent of cellphones, land lines have started to become obsolete, so much so that many telephone operators have medium and long term strategies that only make provision for mobile devices. Even with the advent of Wi-Fi, GSM and UMTS cellphones could soon find themselves overtaken. The larger research institutes throughout the world are in fact trying to establish standards for all wireless communications. This tendency has given rise to hackers that are increasingly specialized in cellphone networks.
There is equipment that is able to «usurp» a victim's connection to the aerial of their operator, and replace them by

acting to all effects like a bridge. These are called fake BTS's [base transceiver stations] and are transportable. For the greater part in white vans (don't ask me why they are white).
The fake BTS's were created around 1997, shortly after the launch of GSM technology, when someone realized that they could no longer listen in on cellphones with a scanner or clock-radio. They were mainly produced in Israel at great expense (about one million dollars, but today they cost slightly less). So these fake BTS's could only be legally bought by police forces and secret services, or perhaps by someone with the right connections and a million dollars in their pocket. But I repeat, to be the object of so much attention, with such a significant outlay, one would have to be really important. Adulterers, people not paying their television subscription and students copying homework can also sleep easy.
Also because, for your information, there are very real risks to the health of whoever listens in using this equipment. For the fake BTS to work properly, it needs to shoot out such a strong signal into the heavens that can supersede any other cellphone aerial in the vicinity, so to dominate your cellphone. Do you know what it means to stand a few centimeters away from a device that shoots out 50 Watts of power in all directions? Well, it literally means getting a tan right down to your bone marrow. In practical terms, it is like standing too close to a small microwave oven, with you taking the part of the main course.
There is another small detail: the device must always be positioned not more than fifty meters away from the objective, which means that our white truck must be positioned right below the house, or the office, or take to following its quarry wherever it goes. Trinity and Bob the Dog experienced the same problem with their Volkswagen panel van:

As soon as Ekström left police headquarters, it was no longer possible to monitor his mobile, unless Trinity knew where he was and could park his van in the immediate vicinity.

>>> The Girl who kicked the hornet's nest, p. 475 (327)

Finally another more pertinent detail: to be able to function as a link, the fake BTS must contain a SIM card from the same operator as the person being tapped. But there is more: so as to not to create suspicion, the caller's number must be displayed on the phone of the person receiving the call. Pretty obvious, no? Not so obvious, because at the outset, they hadn't taken this into consideration. So it happened that some VIP received a call from a strange number. If the call was not taken immediately as can happen to anyone of us, a situation of mild panic would be created inside the van when that person tried to call the number back. Or whoever replied to the call would pose the usual question: «But did you change your number?» «No, why?» Or else: «But which number are you calling from?» «What do you mean?» «Well, I'm not sure… I am getting the number [read out number] displayed» «Mm, not so sure» [suspicious voice].
Again creating panic in the white van that started shaking.
And what if you don't know the number of the person that you want to monitor, but you know for sure that they use a mobile? Trinity and Bob the Dog had to face the same problem:

Trinity and Bob the Dog devoted the best part of a week to identifying and separating out Ekström's mobile from the background noise of about 200,000 other mobile telephones within a kilometer of police headquarters.

>>> The Girl who kicked the hornet's nest, p. 473 (325)

The usual procedure differs somewhat from the one described. Firstly, the fake BTS as we have said does not have a one kilometer range, especially in a city full of recognized telephone operators, because if it did... we'd feel sorry for those people working in the white van!
Secondly, the identifying and separating out of a mobile, must

be done while the person is on the move, in other words, the objective must be followed until it is the only remaining cellphone number that appears on the tapping device's gathering system.

Trinity and Bob the Dog used a technique called Random Frequency Tracking System [RFTS], which had been developed by the American National Security Agency [NSA], and was built in to an unknown number of satellites that performed pinpoint monitoring of the flash points and strategic sites around the world.
The NSA had enormous resources and used a vast network in order to capture a large number of mobile conversations in a certain region simultaneously. Each individual call was separated and processed digitally by computers programmed to react to certain words, such as terrorist or Kalashnikov. If such a word occurred, the computer automatically sent an alarm, which meant that some operator would intervene to decide whether it was of interest or not.

>>> The Girl who kicked the hornet's nest, p. 473 (259)

What has been described may have been possible when cellphones used non digital radio links, especially in the case of encrypted ones. Who can recall the TACS cellphones? You would also then remember that very often by using another appropriate «fake» phone, it was possible to scan for any other casual conversations, but it was very difficult to select a specific one. Sometimes car radios picked up on conversations taking place close to where they were or even television sound. There were also much simpler devices that were very similar to the fake BTS's, simpler in the sense that all they needed to do was tune into the right conversation. Since the introduction of standard GSM's and even with NSA satellites, this is no longer possible. Telephones now use asymmetric encryption (see "Encryptions" in this book), which is very rarely violated by

university researchers and hackers, and then only under very specific circumstances.
It is therefore correct to say that the NSA mainly makes use of its satellites for its own spying and surveillance operations, and that it is extremely difficult for these to be available to a hacker, especially in the case of military operations. It would also be correct to say that the NSA, on behalf of the United States, forms part of the Echelon consortium, together with Great Britain, Canada, Australia and New Zealand. Echelon was the subject of considerable debate and investigation on the part of the European Parliament, especially due to suspicions that is was being used more as a tool for industrial espionage in favor of member State's multinationals, rather than for national security. There are however only a few telephone conversations that go through satellite, while increasing growth is being seen in the use of the Internet as a connection network. The programs tested for word recognition that should direct these conversations to operators for monitoring are still quite sketchy, and when they are utilized often create more false alarms than anything, especially due to the language barrier, seeing that English is not the only language being spoken in the world. Could you imagine a computer existing that was able to collect, analyze and separate millions of telephone calls a minute, in dozens of different languages, while searching for those key words at the same time? It could become a reality in a few decades, but then only if it served some purpose.

It was more difficult to identify a specific mobile telephone. Each mobile has its own unique signature - a kind of fingerprint - in the form of the telephone number.

>>> The Girl who kicked the hornet's nest, p. 473 (325)

Trinity and Bob the Dog probably only want to create some confusion, because the unique signature on a mobile is not actually the telephone number.

What we call a «telephone number» is technically known as a CLI (Calling Line ID, or simply a Caller ID). This is the traditional number assigned by your operator to the «real» telephone number, which is known as the IMSI (International Mobile Subscriber Identity) and is your unique number throughout the world.
A cellphone with a SIM card inserted therefore has two codes that will identify you unequivocally on an international level: the IMSI and the IMEI (International Mobile Equipment Identity), with the latter identifying your cellphone irrespective of the SIM card that has been inserted.
The call tapping that has been ordered by the Authorities is almost always done on the IMSI or the IMEI. Using the IMSI also makes it possible for the identity of whoever is being tapped not to be revealed to the operator that is responsible for the technical side of things. The SIM will be identified on whatever cellphone you decide to install it. Using the IMEI as an interception parameter on the other hand, makes it possible to localize the cellphone regardless of which SIM card has been installed. How many smart alecks think they are secure if they just change their SIM?
Do you really think that Lisbeth would make a similar mistake?

As she waited she removed the SIM card from her telephone and cut it up with some nail scissors. She rolled down the window and tossed out the pieces. Then she took a new SIM card from her wallet and inserted it in her mobile. She was using a Comviq cash card, which was virtually impossible to track. She called Comviq and credited five hundred kroner to the new card.

>>> The Girl who kicked the hornet's nest, p. 854 (597)

She obviously just wanted to create some confusion. What she should have done in this case, besides just destroying the SIM card by cutting it up into little pieces, was to also throw away the cellphone, and then once she had bought a brand new

cellphone using cash, she could have loaded in the new and completely anonymous SIM card.
Let's go back to Trinity and his attempt to listen in on the Judge investigating Lisbeth:

Because Trinity could record the calls from Ekström, he also got voice prints that Plague could process.
Plague ran Ekström's digitized voice through a program called V.P.R.S, Voice print Recognition System. He specified a dozen commonly occurring words such as "okay" and "Salander". When he had five separate examples of a word, he charted it with respect to the time it took Ekström to speak the word, what tone of voice and frequency range it had, whether the end of the word went up or down, and a dozen other markers.

>>> The Girl who kicked the hornet's nest, p. 475 (326-327)

Having their hands on technology able to recognize voice prints with sufficient precision remains a dream of many multi-nationals (and many governments). The preferred usage would be in respect of finding fugitives from justice or terrorists speaking on telephones that have been never been traced on the telephone networks. Another possible application would be on board police cars, including unmarked cars, where they would be used to identify fugitives in public spaces even when they were not speaking on the telephone. Unfortunately this technology is still in the early developmental stages, and whatever is available on the market today does not stretch to these uses.

LANDLINE TAPPING

Things were much simpler on the other hand, with regard to tapping a land line: as long as you knew a technician working for the operator or you had a master key for the small towers or cabinets that are found close to telephone exchanges (even a jimmy would do if you didn't have a master key), you could open them up and attach a recorder or radio transmitter on the connection you needed, and spend the rest of the day listening in or come past at the end of the day to retrieve the recorder. Try to imagine how many records or transmitters have been discovered in Italy over the last ten years. A few hundred. And according to statistics, and in the best of Italian traditions, most of these refer to cases of marital infidelity.

.

CALLING ON THE INTERNET

Things are changing with the advent of the Internet, because almost all land line and mobile calls are ultimately channeled onto a VoIP [voice over Internet protocol] line or something similar, and any decent hacker with a good grip of the network, can listen in and record them from anywhere he wants. VoIP has taken wiretapping to a new level: it is definitely impossible to use traditional methods (recorder in the cabinet, white panel van, etcetera), and only someone with an inkling of IT pitched somewhere above the average can institute a VoIP interception. These people are able to listen in and record a call connected to the Internet from the other side of the world, and in extreme cases, all the traffic from a specific area can be routed through a specific Cyberworld point simply by manipulating the so-called «routing tables». In simple terms, these are the routing instructions that are given to all communications leaving your computer or PDA.

Hands up whoever uses Skype. And you feel more secure using Skype. I wouldn't be so sure: there are a number of ways to intercept a Skype communication between users, and even without these, the telephone operators providing incorporated Skype services have included such powerful probes on their network that they are able to capture and record any traffic that is generated by their clients. As we have seen, services like tapping are defined as the «mandatory rendering of services», given that the telephone operator works under license. These services are obviously available to the Judicial Authorities, but the people managing these services are still just people: who's to say that they won't succumb to the temptation of abusing their position?

A frequent question is how do you know when you are being listened to? It's definitely not going to be by having a chat with the policeman, or trying to make out the background noise or coughing fit that would betray whoever is listening in on you. You should start getting suspicious if you can't make a call even when the lines are free, or if the call is cut off once too often in the middle of a conversation. We're looking at a different scenario when dealing with fake BTS's. Your call can be affected by significant disturbances due to the proximity and strength of the transmitting aerial, and also because it serves as a go-between you and whoever you are calling.

The only way to avoid having your telephone calls tapped is not to have a cellphone. Something to think about…

DO YOU FEEL YOU ARE BEING WATCHED?

CRYPTOGRAPHY

The ancient Romans were probably the first to use cryptography (hidden writing) as a way of creating secure lines of communication over their expansive empire, given the priority of communicating between the capital and outlying areas. One of the first known systems was created by Julius Caesar, where each letter in the text was replaced by a letter one or two position further up the alphabet. Although quite simple, this method is still used effectively today when youngsters try to avoid the messages they send on to their friends from being immediately apparent to their parents. An expert in cryptography though would have little trouble in identifying the key. The «key» is the series of instructions that would allow the hidden message to be revealed, and in this case it would refer to the number used to replace each letter. Let's look at an example: word in plain text: "mamma"; encrypted word: "nbnnb". In this case the key is +1.
This system has been developed further, for example by allocating a different value to the first, second and third letter, and then going back to the first. In this case the word «mamma» would become: "ncpnc", and the key would be: (1)+1, (2)+2, (3)+3.
Over time, cryptography methods reached increased levels of

complexity and sophistication, culminating in the Enigma system used by the Nazis in the Second World War, where the Allies were able to anticipate the German's code by breaking the code. Enigma formed the cornerstone for the establishment of the famous NSA (National Security Agency), which went on to become the richest and most powerful spy agency in the world. The Second World War was therefore won on the basis of intelligence gathering rather than brute force, in other words using the same unconventional systems adopted by Lisbeth and professional hackers. In order to prevent the Japanese from decoding their messages, the Americans went as far as conscripting Navajo Indians (so-called Wind Talkers) and using their ethnic language to transmit information. From the Cold War onwards, cryptography took center stage when it came to secrets that needed to be protected, and the advent of Cyberworld and computers increased its power, making it a technology that was available to the masses. France, for example, considers cryptography to be on a par with tactical weapons, and its use in France has been banned by Law. The United States allows its companies to export cryptographic software only if a master access key is made available to the NSA. Two people were arrested in England in 2009, because they refused to provide the password to open certain private documents following a casual check on their computers.

Modern cryptography is referred to as «asymmetrical», where it contains two keys, a public and private key. The public key is made available to everyone that we exchange encrypted documents with, while the private key is ours alone. Together the private key, public key and password will open a document that is addressed to us.

One of the first encryption systems made available to hackers by the underground was PGP (Pretty Good Privacy). This is the same one that was usually used by Lisbeth.

She added her PGP key, encrypted the email with the Plague's PGP key and pressed Send. She then checked

the time and saw that it was just past half past seven in the evening.

> > > *The Girl who played with fire, p. 40*

Once she has written the email, Lisbeth uses PGP to encrypt the document and, seeing that it is addressed to Plague, she adds her public key to the system. On receiving the message, he can open and read it using his private key. The message is therefore only addressed to Plague, and he is the only one that can open it. The public and private key system, or asymmetric cryptography overrides the need for people to speak or communicate with each other in order to exchange keys. Naturally this system also has a fundamental weak spot: namely the human factor.

Do you remember what was said about the war between Telecom and Kroll? The stupidity and casual approach of one person nullified all the security procedures of the large private investigation multinational, and made it possible for hackers to gain free access to all the systems, documents, electronic mail and diaries of dozens of operating agents. Food for thought: the Kroll agents also made use of PGP. Guess where they kept their private and public keys: in the computer, of course. The first thing hackers do when they access a computer or network is to get all the user names and passwords, and if the computer or network password is the same as the PGP, then its a piece of cake.

Lisbeth wouldn't have acted any differently in this case, as she considered stupidity a far greater sin than keeping any unconfessed secret. At first, it may seem strange that Lisbeth and her friends encrypt insignificant messages, containing no confidential information.

When Lisbeth checked her inbox, she found four messages. The first was from Plague and had been sent about an hour after she had written to him. The message was encrypted and contained three words asking a terse question. Are you alive?

Plague was never one for writing long sentimental messages. But then, the same was true of Lisbeth.
Both subsequent emails had been sent at around two in the morning. The first was again from Plague, with encrypted information telling of a virtual acquaintance that went by the name of Bilbo and happened to live in Texas, who had picked up on her request. Plague had attached the address and PGP key. A couple of minutes later, Bilbo had sent her a message from a hotmail address. The message was brief and saying only that the information on Doctor Forbes would be forwarded within the next twenty four hours.

>>> The Girl who played with fire, p. 71

So here is something important that Plague, Lisbeth and any other hacker worth their salt does, and which should become common practice in both the private or institutional domain where cryptography is essential for protecting secrets. Once cryptography is being used, it must be used for everything, not only for secrets. If we only use it for secrets, we are highlighting to anyone searching, exactly where to find the worthwhile information. So they in turn will concentrate their efforts only on getting the access key, by trying to find someone that is guilty of a casual approach and stupidity.
There is another trick that Lisbeth also probably uses on the quiet: everyone knows that every file has an extension to its name indicating what kind of file it is, which suggests to the computer which program it should use to open it. For example: Word documents carry the extension .doc, Excel .xls, and some files containing images are marked as .jpg etcetera.
Documents that have been encrypted using PGP carry a .pgp or .pgd extension and it therefore makes it easy for a hacker, or anyone to conduct a search for this type of document. When you have real secrets, you must change the extension on the file.
More recently another encryption method has become

widespread, which started off as a method used many years before the existence of computers: namely steganography. Using a specific program, a hacker can take a message and hide it in a multimedia file like a photo, or video etcetera. Whoever knows where to look, opens the same file with a specific program, keys in the password and our message appears as if by magic. The beauty of this system is that you don't have to send the file via email, you can just post the image or photo on a website, like YouTube.

Finally, let's look at another innovation called «Deniable Cryptography». If someone finds themselves in a no-win situation, with someone pointing a gun at their head to get them to reveal the password for an encrypted document, any cryptography is going to be useless. This technology has been developed around the use of two or more passwords, so that the first would open the actual environment with real information, while the second opens a simulated environment with various documents, but these do not contain any of the secrets that need protecting.

I'll let you in to another secret, which is known by few in the underground and originates from the Navajo Wind Talkers during the Second World War: some hacker groups don't even bother with cryptography to speak on the phone or when they exchange emails, but prefer to use unknown and often invented languages taken from fiction. For example, Klingon that was spoken by the mythical alien race in Star Trek or Sindarin, the elves' language in Lord of the Rings. There are dictionaries available for these languages in Anglo-Saxon countries, and people have simply taken to studying and learning them. Can you imagine listening in on a telephone call conducted in Klingon? Would there be a sworn interpreter available to translate it?

RFID: TECH RECORDS AND MONEY

Until as recently as twenty years ago, documents were printed out on paper, and so any procedure that identified a citizen of a country was in paper form. This also meant that they could easily be falsified and were difficult to verify on a cursory check.
Today we find ourselves in a hybrid position, and so it is still possible to «disappear» like Lisbeth did when she was being hunted down:

Through this network she could also find herself hide-outs abroad.. It had been Plague's contacts on the Net who had provided her with a Norwegian passport in the name of Irene Nesser.

>>> The Girl who kicked the hornet's nest, p. 386 (259)

False documents, and a new identity. Disappear from view and start up a new life. How many of us haven't imagined doing this at least once? Pity it's so damn difficult to achieve outside of a criminal context.
And yet, in a few years time not even criminals will be able to achieve this, unless they are exceptional hackers, and

international systems still have some flaw to exploit. In fact, technology is taking the whole concept of identification to levels of obscurity that were never dreamed of regarding a person's privacy. Remember that everything has its dark side.
Disappearing today using falsified documents and a new identity would only be possible under very limited circumstances: with documents from a third-world country, where procedures are still quite backward. Or if your government provided you with a «new life» for security reasons; something that happens only rarely and under circumstances that it would be better not to know too much about.
«RFID» (Radio Frequency Identification) is a technology that has been used more extensively over recent years. It functions with a transponder containing data and a reader that prompts the transponder to communicate this data.
If anyone has traveled to the United States recently, you would know that this requires a special passport, containing a mandatory transponder in which all your personal details are stored, together with other information called up from the data bank of whoever is checking the documents. These are often connected to international data banks that could contain other information about you.
Swipe cards used in companies, on public transport, for health services and any other device read electronically will more than often function with this technology for a very simple and practical reason: wherever you go, all you need to do is go through a barrier, or come near the relevant reader, and all information contained in the transponder that you are carrying with you, is instantly transmitted and you become traceable.
During DEFCON, one of the most significant conferences for underground hackers in the world, a group of professional hackers gave the entire world an impressive demonstration of this system. Mindful of the extensive use of systems using transponders carrying personal details, and especially of the fact that a large number of undercover agents from the American Federal Authorities, Secret Service and Armed

Forces would be attending, the hackers positioned an indistinct pole in an area frequented by everyone. Unbeknown to anyone, the pole contained a powerful RFID reader. The reader immediately took to scanning the surrounding area searching for any information contained on swipe cards or documents. After a while this was then linked up to a maxi-screen visible to everyone in the area, which began screening the data that had already been lifted, and what was being received in real time. To the amazement of the crowd, the screen started displaying the swipe cards of FBI agents, Navy, State Department, secret services and police personnel, as well as those belonging to people out of uniform that were carrying any kind of electronic badge.

The hacker's decision in providing the authorities with this startling and embarrassing demonstration was to show how this situation touches our lives, and everything that identifies us and where it should be up to us whether or not we want to disclose any single bit of this information. Well, it seems that technology is being used to deprive us of this very power, and Lisbeth and her hacker friends have only one response to try and invalidate this inexorable flow: by making it public and known to everyone, in the same way that any other vulnerability in information systems is exploited.

RFID readers can quite easily be adapted to devices like the most ordinary PDAs. So all you need to do is hop on the a bus, or go into a restaurant or cinema, activate the reader, and you can identify everyone within a radius of a few meters. But that is not all: if your heath card contains a transponder, that information will also be transmitted, in the same way as the information on your card for public transport or your favorite shopping haunt. If your credit card has been updated with this technology, then even this will no longer remain a secret.

Can you just imagine what somebody malicious could do with his hands on one of these readers?

That's not the end of it though.

Let's take a look at the Euro, that invaluable currency commonly used throughout our dear old Europe. All Euro banknotes contain a transponder, which identifies them and contains certain basic information, like the amount and serial number. When some people started asking questions and trying to document things, they discovered that the Euro was designed in a way that it could be identified by a RFID reader, as a tool in the fight against kidnappings with ransom demands and such like.

But there are also many people who believe that a real monster has been created. Can you just imagine going through a checkpoint at the airport, or anywhere in town where a reader is placed, as for example at the entrance to limited traffic areas (where it is hidden so that it does not rouse suspicion), or at a tollgate on the highway, and stop to consider that this checkpoint contains a RFID reader. Well, not only will all the information contained on your electronic documents be read, but the actual money you have in your pocket will also be accessed.

Now imagine what our same malicious person with the PDA reader could do while passing you on the street and gaining access to everything there is to know about you. Or even the crook that breaks into your house and office, who would be able to find your money at the bat of an eyelid. It seems that organized crime has been provided with a convenient method for picking their victims.

Some underground investigators have found a surefire method for checking whether a RFID exists on bank notes. They simply place a note in a microwave oven, as if you were warming up a cup of milk and let it turn a few times. If it's done properly, then you should see a small flame coming off the bank note that will leave a tiny hole. This marks the position of the RFID.

From 2008, some keen observers have even started picking up RFID's on the American 20 dollar notes.

Luckily, professionals like Lisbeth are comfortable navigating the murky waters of Cyberworld. Finding the information with an RFID reader and replicating it is not an impossible feat for a hacker. But where does that leave the man on the street.

Worse still, can you imagine what this technology could mean in the hands of organizations like those run by the Nigerians or the Russian Business Network?

BIG BANK

Could you even imagine a world without banks? Perhaps those of you with a more Utopian view of life could, but in reality the whole food chain of our society has been built around banks, making it impossible to circumvent them. Everyone «has» to have a bank account and credit line, and if our bank decides to take that away from us, we could be ruined with a single click. Even the talk of control strategies on a global level, with the plausible excuses of money laundering, tax fraud, financing of terrorism and what have you, tend to enmesh every citizen in the stranglehold of the banks, to the point where we are forced to hold an account and conduct every payment we make through them. How many of you have ever wondered what happens to your money when it gets to the bank? Perhaps some of you imagine it ending up in a specially labeled coffer with your name on it. But in reality, whatever the extent of our riches, our money magically becomes a simple number inside a data bank. And naturally whatever this number may be, it lives inside the vulnerabilities of the computer and networks, where it is susceptible to the faults and flaws of humans.

We have a lot to fear, but there are two instances we should fear the most if we exclude the possibility of the Government

itself denying us access to our small or larger fortune as the case may be. The first would be the actions carried out by the bank itself on the data bank, and the second would be the stealing of our identity.
In the first instance, we can keep our fingers crossed and hope that nothing ever happens. But in the second, we can be proactive if we just pay a little more attention.
Let's take a look at what Lisbeth did with her friend Mikael:

«I am not kidding. I need to borrow 120 000 kroner for – let's say – six weeks. I have a chance to make an investment, but I don't have anyone else to turn to. You've got roughly 140 000 kroner in your current account right now. You'll get your money back.»
No point commenting on the fact that Salander had hacked his bank password and taken a look at how much he had in his account. It was obvious that he was using Internet banking.

>>> The Girl with the dragon tattoo, pp. 641-642 (503)

It's all too easy for Lisbeth to check on Mikael's bank account from the minute that she had gained access to the contents on his computer. Naturally the same thing applies to using banking services on the Internet, where we are not identified in a physical sense, but on the basis of our cyber identity. This could either be through a username and password, or digital certificate, or secret code or whatever. Whoever has access to our computer, also has complete access to what we are doing. Any decent Trojan Horse could be instructed to recognize the keying in of credentials in the relevant boxes when we have accessed a «secure» site. From the minute a hacker has stolen your banking identity, the system will allow him to do anything, as if you were doing it yourself.
Over time, organized crime has come to depend on hackers and has formalized these transactions, giving rise to a new threat known as «phishing». This term refers to the process of

attempting to gain sensitive information from unsuspecting people through the net, using social engineering techniques applied to Internet communications.
The phisher throws out a hook into the net, by accessing the large amount of email addresses he has at his disposal, and sending a message designed to look like an official bank or public administration office, down to the smallest detail including the sender's address. From the minute we open the message, we have already signaled to our phisher that our email address is active and being used by someone. We are then requested for reasons that initially seem quite plausible, to enter our details in the relevant spaces or to link onto a site, which seems identical to the original one and log in our access codes. At the end of the operation, the site confirms that you have followed instructions and everything seems to be in order. But, from that moment onwards, anything that you revealed to the phisher (your credit card number with secret codes, username and password to access your online account, etcetera), will be used to rob you. This may initially be done in smaller amounts so as not to raise any suspicions that something is amiss on your account.
When you do finally realize what is happening, all you can do is report it. From then onwards you will be protected against further damage, but whatever disappeared before will be lost, because all clients are responsible for the use that is made of their banking credentials and cyber identity.
It is actually quite simple to defend yourself from phishing: don't ever open email messages that seem to come from banking institutions or public administration offices. If you do happen to open them, remember that no bank will ever ask you to disclose any of your credentials or sensitive details via email.
Obviously the situation is quite different in Mikael's case: his credentials were lifted directly from his computer using a Trojan Horse, and luckily Lisbeth is his friend.
It's worth spending a little more time on the question of banking fraud. The formalization of this business by organized

criminals that use hackers, largely benefits from the protocol of transferring information that the international banking system uses. As we have already noted, almost all the information that one bank transfers to another refers to a sum of money. Remember that in the bank, your money is transformed into a simple number sitting inside a data bank. We could refer to a protocol as a standard language that machines use to communicate between themselves. The language most commonly used by banks is called X25.

X25 was developed during the seventies, and it can be considered the forerunner of all subsequent communication protocols, including the one used by the Internet today. There are very few technicians that know the system well because it has come to be considered obsolete and inadequate in relation to the use that is made of net today. Well now, the largest concentration of X25 experts is to be found in Russia, and many of these are hackers that serve in organizations like the Russian Business Network. The banks are those with the most to fear from these kinds of attacks, because the sectors that are most often hit are those involved in the transfer of funds between banking institutions.

Lisbeth organized a huge fraud against the infamous magnate Wennerström, which the Russian Business Network would probably have carried out using its X25 experts. After infiltrating his computer, she is able to track the financial transactions.

Lisbeth worked in a trance-like state. The account – click – email– click – balance sheets – click. She noted down the latest transfers. She tracked a small transaction from Japan to Singapore and on via Luxembourg to the Cayman Islands. She understood how it worked. It was as if she were part of the impulses in cyberspace. Small changes. The latest e-mail. One brief message of peripheral interest was sent at 10.00 p.m. The PGP encryption program rattle, rattle, was a joke for anyone who was already inside his computer and could read the

message in plain text.

>>> The Girl with the dragon tattoo, pp. 638-639 (500-501)

Lisbeth has total control over her victim's PC, and needs nothing further. Ingenuously, all his credentials are lying there in plain sight of the hacker, including his PGP key allowing access to his encrypted messages.
In actual fact, off shore banks never allow online banking for reasons of «confidentiality». But they could allow a user to issue instructions via email and this is where Lisbeth was able to follow the various transfers of money between the myriad of accounts controlled by the infamous magnate.
A final suggestion to all those who are not magnates. Wherever possible, try not to keep too much money in your current account. Always ask for iron-clad guarantees from your bank when using Internet banking, and until you are assured of these or you are not yet up to speed with the potential dangers, rather stick with traditional banking methods. Luckily traditional bank robberies don't affect the money held in your account!

EPILOGUE: THE PARABLE OF THE DARK SIDE

One day the President of the United States was busy watching the Pope deliver an address on television. The Pope ended with a message directed to the whole world: «There will be peace in the world when the Lion lies with the Lamb».

The President took the Pope's pronouncement seriously and called his Cabinet, entrusting them with the project of solving the problem of world peace.

All kinds of experts, Nobel laureates, gurus in politics and strategists were called on, with the United Nations and many others, who all worked tirelessly for years on this ambitious project set by the President.

One fine day, a commission of experts presented their results to the Cabinet and the President, satisfied with the outcome, declared that the project had been concluded.

A press conference was immediately called to report the good news to the media.

Alerted to this worldwide broadcast, the Pope switched on his television set as the President was about to begin.

«We set ourselves an objective and we dedicated huge resources so that a final solution could be found to world

peace.»
Journalists and television networks were aware of the significance of what the President was about to reveal and everyone held their breath waiting to learn the secret.
«Under the auspices of the United States of America, we gathered the highest minds in the world, who worked tirelessly to resolve the most significant problem of all time.»
Everyone was caught up in the emotion of the moment, and those following the event on television moved closer to the screen so that they could witness this momentous announcement.
Even the Pope held his breath, and leaned further forward in his armchair in rapt attention.
«But words are worthless. I would now like to unveil a work of art.»
The President signaled to someone off screen and the cameras zoomed over to a curtain that opened.
There in front of the eyes of the fascinated spectators and television audience, was an enormous lion with a sweet little lamb cuddled up on its stomach.
The Pope could not believe his eyes, and decided to head for Washington to see this miracle wrought by the President of the United States, with his own eyes.
On his arrival in Washington, the Pope was escorted to the location of the miracle and saw the enormous lion cuddled up with the lamb for himself.
The Pope could not contain his emotions, and thanked the President for what he had achieved, asking him the secret of this miracle.
The President smiled.
«In actual fact, the solution was always right before our very eyes.»
The Pope listened on intently and asked.
«Please Mr. President, what was the secret?»
The President hesitated for a moment, but then decided that the world should know the truth.
«It's very simple», he said. «A lamb a day.»

Whatever we have or are given, or just take for granted comes at a price, which all too often we pretend not to know, averting our eyes so that we do not look too closely. There is a village in Africa that feeds a pack of hyenas on daily basis, to ensure that they don't trespass into the village and prey on its inhabitants. All the well-being and progress that technology brings with it comes at a high price: firstly our identity, and then our privacy in the most extreme scenario. Whatever we have gained thanks to technology, can just as easily be taken away, starting with our money and ending with our very identity. It could become so easy in the future to strip everything from a person by simply pressing a button. Without even stopping to think of our private lives. Technology exacts our life in return, and it's important that we are cognizant that this is a road with no return.

In a world living by these rules, there are minds that are able to dominate technology and exploit its weaknesses, especially its most basic vulnerability: the human factor. Einstein said that «the difference between genius and stupidity is that genius has its limits». We will have to wait and see what stupidity can do when it's combined with the exponential power of technology.

And so we reveal the secret of reality hiding behind appearances. Our sense of calm fills us with a sense of security, but this is only true on the surface. We prefer not to look too closely at the underlying chaos and we willingly pay the price, because its actually better not to look or feel , but rather continue on in the blissful ignorance of the living coma we call life.

And then one day along comes Lisbeth, and nothing is ever the same.

GLOSSARY

Wi- fi Access Point
Access point to a wireless network. Access Points can be private if they are for household use, or public, if they belong to a telephone operator and are available to enabled users to the Internet.

ADSL
It stands for «Asymmetric Digital Subscriber Line» and it is a technology for the exchange of information that allows faster transmission over copper telephone lines than the old telephone lines.

Al-electronic al-jihad
2000 Manifesto, attributed to Osama bin Laden that marks the beginning of the holy war in Cyberworld.

Cache
Storage space on a hard disk, where temporary data is stored, as for example the images contained on a web page that has been opened.

Trojan or Trojan Horse

Type of computer virus that allows a hacker to access an infected computer and carry out various operations.

CLI (Calling Line Id, or simply Caller ID)

A telephone number

Zombie Computer

A computer infected by a dormant virus waiting on instructions from a hacker. The infection usually happens through an email prepared by the hacker and sent indiscriminately to thousands of email addresses. When a zombie is activated, the hacker generally instructs it to attack other computers so as to saturate the bandwidth thereby obstructing normal connections to the Internet.

Cyberworld

Neologism identifying the complete range of virtual dimensions within the Internet.

DefCon

It stands for «Defense Condition», and it is the official term used by the American government to indicate the various levels of a national emergency. It's also the name of one of the most well-known conferences for hackers held in Las Vegas.

DMZ

Demilitarized zone. A real or virtual place where no conflict is allowed by agreement of all parties involved.

DoS

Denial of Service. A kind of hacker attack, which blocks communications on the Internet to a computer or entire network.

Exploit

Computer program created especially for exploiting a known

or unknown vulnerability in a software or hardware.

Fake BTS (Base Transceiver Station)

It literally means fake radio base station. These are mobile devices that are almost identical to the real «aerials» that cellphones are connected to. They are administered by private entities rather than telephone operators, and are almost always used for wiretapping There is another type, which is widely used. This does not intercept, but identifies all the cellphones present in a specific area, and wherever possible, links them to the name of the holders.

Firewall

Boundary device protecting a computer or network.

GPS (Global Positioning System)

American military system for localizing objects, formulated from a network of geo-stationary satellites. Like the Internet, GPS was conceived as a military system, and then came to be used in a civilian context.

Hack Meetings

Meetings between hackers from all over the world, where they learn of new attack methods, circulate new vulnerabilities and organize competitions to violate specific computers.

Hostile takeover

Infiltrate a computer or network and take control of it.

IMEI (International Mobile Equipment Identity)

Numeric code transmitted on the cellphone network that unequivocally identifies the phone on an international level

IMSI (International Mobile Subscriber Identity)

Unique number at an international level that represents the real telephone number linked to a SIM card.

IP Address (Internet Protocol)
Code made up of four groups of three figures that identify the connection of a computer on the network.

ISP (Internet Service Provider)
A structure or company providing access services to the Internet for users.

Mainframe
Term that today identifies a mega-computer servicing a large corporation, which hosts critical information and applications.

Malware
Software created to damage a computer or network, or exploit some vulnerability in favor of the instigators.

Override Category
One of the terms used to identify telephones that can see all incoming numbers, even when are hidden.

Skilled
Someone with talent.

Spy-Ops
Spy operations

Spyware
Software created for spying or intercepting data and communications.

Routing tables
Files that contain routing information, in other words the route that a communication must take from the address it originates from to its destination.

TACS (Total Access Communication System)

Cellphone system prior to GSM with analogue functioning.

UMTS (Universal Mobile Telecommunication System)
Also known as 3G, or third generation system. A technology for cellphone telecommunications with aspirations to become the single world standard.

Underground
Indicates the information technology borderline zone, usually occupied by hackers.

VoIP (Voice over Internet Protocol)
Telephony system that transforms telephone calls into data packages, which travel on the Internet up to their destination, where they again become voice.

VPN (Virtual Private Network)
A virtual private network usually encrypted and used for secure communications.

Wannabe
American slang deriving from want to be. In computers, indicative of people who would like to be hackers, but are lacking the talent and attributes.

Wind Talkers
Native American Indians from the Navajo tribe, who collaborated during the Second World War, using their native language to relay messages between central command and troops on the front, as this was incomprehensible to the Japanese.

WPA (Wi-Fi Protected Access)
Protection system for Wi-Fi connections, breached for the first time in 2009 and therefore no longer so secure.

. . .

ABOUT THE AUTHOR

Fabio Ghioni was born in Milano, Italy, sometime in the 20th century. He majored a PhD in Clinical Psychology and is recognized as one of the major pioneers of the digital age although most of his work for governments cannot be disclosed or even mentioned. He was asked to write a book on hacking and he chose to do it in a simple language to reach anybody and not just skilled techies. He always says that the best antivirus and the best firewall is the human brain when used.

Besides being one of the greatest minds of unconventional technologies he is also a lecturer, journalist and novelist and in 2012 he founded the Evolution and New Order Civilization Project and the Philosophy of Apotheosis.

For more information:

progetto.enoc@gmail.com

www.ingramcontent.com/pod-product-compliance
Lightning Source LLC
LaVergne TN
LVHW092336060326
832902LV00008B/665
* 9 7 8 1 5 2 0 7 3 2 5 0 3 *